The Legend of Bernardo del Carpio
From Chronicle to Drama

Scripta Humanistica

Directed by
BRUNO M. DAMIANI
The Catholic University of America

The Legend of Bernardo del Carpio
From Chronicle to Drama

David G. Burton

Foreword by
John Lihani

Scripta humanistica

47

Burton, David G.
The legend of Bernardo del Carpio from chronicle to drama / David G. Burton.
p. cm. — (Scripta Humanistica : 47)
Bibliography : p.
ISBN 0-196379-54-X : $30.00
1. Cueva. Juan de la, 1550?-1610? Libertad de España por Bernardo del Carpio. 2. Bernardo del Carpio (Legendary character) in literature. I. Title. II. Series : Scripta Humanistica (Series) ; 47.
PQ6388.C9B434 1989
862'.3—dc19 88-39322
CIP

Publisher and Distributor:
SCRIPTA HUMANISTICA
1383 Kersey Lane
Potomac, Maryland 20854 U.S.A.

Library of Congress Catalog Card Number 88-39322
International Standard Book Number 0-916379-54-X

Table of Contents

Acknowledgments

I extend my deepest gratitude and appreciation to the following people who have helped me in the preparation of this study:

To John Lihani, mentor and friend, who has so kindly written the preface, and who has given so consistently of his endless patience, encouragement, and interest in me and in the progress of this study.

To Judge James Baskin whose appreciation of and respect for the English language continues to inspire me.

To Bruno Damiani who saw the merits of the text and encouraged its publication.

To Debbie Lloyd who, with unfaltering eye, proofread the typescript.

To my mother whose love, patience, and faith over the years have served as a model.

Foreword

The flowering of the Spanish drama in the period known as the Golden Age was the result of a long dramatic tradition that went as far back as the Greek and Roman Classical period. Even before the fall of the Roman Empire in the fifth century A.D., Spain had acquired the role of custodian of the Roman civilization in the Iberian Peninsula, where ultimately the arts of the Western world collided with those of the Eastern, during the centuries of occupation by the Arabs. With renewed assimilation of world learning, from the medieval period through the Renaissance and up to the eighteenth century, Spain continued to make contributions in the sciences and the arts as one of the leading cultural forces of the world.

It was particularly during the sixteenth century that the Spanish theater made its enormous formative strides, both in the secular and religious vein. It was then, at a time when the ancient Classical tradition and the exuberance of the folk drama was ready to merge with the insights of the recent techniques of the early Spanish playwrights, that Juan de la Cueva came on the scene. The notable practice of the histrionic art by the early Spanish playwrights of the Salamancan school, such as Fernando de Rojas, Juan del Encina, Lucas Fernández, and Bartolomé de Torres Naharro, among many others, had begun to crystallize the national direction for the Spanish stage. By the end of the sixteenth century, the Spanish drama occupied an important place on the world stage with its consolidation of native themes through the efforts of one of its stellar figures, Juan de la Cueva.

With the participation of Juan de la Cueva, the Spanish theater experienced a definite trend towards cultivation of national topics. Cueva's fourteen extant plays payed homage to the venerable past, but struck a new chord, bringing on significant changes in dramatic content and techniques.

The plays became the vehicle for events that reflected the very spirit of the people.

As professor David Burton clearly points out in the following chapters of his book, Juan de la Cueva was particularly influential in steering the path of the Spanish drama toward the development of native historical themes. He became, in fact, a presenter of personalized history. Cueva's dramatic talent seized upon historical figures and related them to contemporary leaders who were cause for concern to Cueva's intellectual and political posture.

Dr. Burton takes a new look at the *Comedia de la libertad de España por Bernardo del Carpio,* and points out Cueva's innovative art as it is manifested in this work. He takes an outstanding example of Cueva's historical themes, here based upon the events of the legendary medieval hero, Bernardo del Carpio, and clarifies the influential role that Cueva's dramatic art played in the formulation of the Spanish *comedia* of the seventeenth century.

Professor Burton further demonstrates in this first complete study of the *Comedia de la libertad de España por Bernardo del Carpio* that Cueva went beyond the mere presentation of the legendary hero's victory over Charlemagne's French army at Roncesvalles. One of the interesting and important aspects of Burton's treatise is that he shows that Cueva imbued his play with several levels of meaning in a manner that is not generally associated with Spanish sixteenth-century plays. The author-critic affirms that it can be read on the first, or peripheral, level as an exaltation and as an exultation of a national hero; on a second inner level as a political allegory of Philip II's attempt to add Portugal to the Spanish crown; and on a third level, as a triumph of virtue over vice; and finally at the innermost, core level, it can be read as a focus on faith, in which forgiveness and the promise of redemption follow the repentance for sin.

Dr. Burton provides a most welcome monograph with a fresh appraisal of Cueva's dramatic art. He delineates the playwright's contributions to the forward movement of the theater in Spain, noting the innovations that Cueva brought to the Spanish stage, as he adapted the historical material to the demanding cultural taste of his audience.

The rise of the national theater of the Golden Age hinged upon the various features from the Classical tradition, combined with aspects taken from the popular theater, and formulated by the techniques evolved by the Salamancan school of dramatists. All these elements needed to be assimilated and thence transmitted in their essence to the incomparably prolific group of playwrights who were to cluster later around the brilliance of

Lope de Vega. As Professor Burton maintains, the primary transmitter, the pivotal link between the sixteenth century's tradition and innovation and the Golden Age's supreme dramatic productions was the talented master of the budding national theater, Juan de la Cueva.

John Lihani
University of Kentucky

Prologue

Juan de la Cueva is an important dramatist in the Spanish theater prior to Lope de Vega. His innovations in dramatic writing are readily apparent in the third of his plays based on Spanish history, *La libertad de España por Bernardo del Carpio*. This play, although often cited by Spanish literary historians, is virtually unstudied and has been overlooked until the 1970s.

The play is important because it reveals Cueva's art as a dramatist and his influential role as a precursor of the Spanish theater of the seventeenth century. Cueva's creativity, which proved to be effective, is demonstrated in aspects of his writing style and in his desire to teach and to advocate. Cueva was the first Spanish dramatist to use Spanish history for subject matter, and the first to use polymetric verse throughout a play. In addition, Cueva appears to be among the early Spanish playwrights to break with the unities of place and time and to use drama as a tool for more than simple entertainment, for advocacy.

In this study, an attempt is made to provide an initial examination of Cueva's dramatization of the ancient legend of Bernardo del Carpio. This project has been divided into six chapters. In the first, Cueva's life and works are discussed briefly. The author was influenced, both as a person and as a writer, by the ambience of his native Seville. The legend of Bernardo del Carpio is presented in the second chapter. Similarities and differences between the three thirteenth-century chronicle accounts and the sixteenth-century version of the life of Bernardo are pointed out. In addition, the ballad and epic traditions which also treat the hero's life and deeds are explored. In Chapter Three the plot of the drama is told, major variances from history are described, and Cueva's stylistic techniques are examined. In Chapter Four, the characters in the play are analyzed. Chapter Five explores the play as an entertainment device. Chapter Six attempts to uncover the thematic structure of the play.

Chapter I
The Life and Works of Juan de la Cueva

Juan de la Cueva, a remarkable sixteenth-century Spanish playwright, was possessed of an appreciation of the history of his country as well as the cultural, political, and religious tides of his native Seville in his own day. Combining these attributes with a keen sense of drama, he was the first Spanish dramatist to utilize Spain's medieval chronicles and rich ballad tradition as source material for dramatic stories. He was also the first to break out of the constraints of the rules of composition relating to the unities of time and place. Following the precedent set by Bartolomé de Torres Naharro, Cueva made use of words, accents, and action appropriate to a given situation. Finally, he pioneered the use of drama for teaching and for advocacy.

Cueva used historical fact and tradition to encourage political and patriotic action and to make moral and religious statements. In so doing, he is a singularly important link in the evolutionary chain of the Spanish national drama prior to Lope de Vega. It is the confluence of his use of chronicled history, of his decorous writing, and of his advocacy and persuasion in *Comedia de la libertad de España por Bernardo del Carpio* which provided the stimulus for this study.[1]

---

[1] *Comedia de la libertad de España por Bernardo del Carpio* is the least studied of Cueva's three plays based on popular, legendary tales from Spanish history. The following authors present thumbnail summaries and evaluations:

Edwin S. Morby, "The Plays of Juan de la Cueva," Diss. University of California 1936, pp. 77-80.

In order that Cueva's views and motivations may be understood — or at least made the subject of reasonable inference — a brief consideration of his life, of his place within an historical continuum, and of his works is in order. Biographical data pertaining to this sixteenth-century Spanish dramatist and poet, at best sketchy, are difficult to find. Until very recently researchers had failed to uncover Cueva's baptism and burial certificates, and had relied on the scholarship of the nineteenth-century Swedish Hispanist Fredrik Wulff, who, in 1886, postulated Cueva's birth to have been around the year 1550 in Seville.[2] Then, in 1980, José María Reyes Cano found and published Cueva's baptismal certificate which places his birth in the early fall of 1543.[3]

Although many other exact dates in Juan de la Cueva's life are missing, Cueva himself supplies various pieces of the biographical puzzle throughout his works. In the genealogical poem *Historia y sucesión de la Cueva* (1604) Juan de la Cueva narrates the history of his noble family from the fifteenth century when King Henry IV made Beltrán de la Cueva the first Duke of Alburquerque.[4] In the conclusion of the poem Cueva praises his father, Martín López de la Cueva, his six sisters, and his one brother, Claudio. He also exhibits pride in his renowned cousins Andrés Zamudio de Alfaro, a physician to King Philip II, who wrote a treatise on Seville's pestilence of 1568,[5] and

---

Francisco E. Porrata, *Incorporación del romancero a la temática de la comedia española* (Madrid: Editorial Playor, 1973), pp. 124-59.

Richard F. Glenn, *Juan de la Cueva* (New York: Twayne Publishers, 1973), pp. 64-9. Hereafter Glenn.

[2] Fredrik A. Wulff, "Poèmes inédits de Juan de la Cueva," *Lunds Universitets Ars-skrift,* 23 (1886-87), p. xlvi. "Cela est vrai, mais plus j'étudie ses écrits, plus je me persuade qu'il y aurait moins d'inconvênients à placer sa naissance entre 1545 et 1550 qu'en 1550-52." Hereafter Wulff.

[3] José María Reyes Cano, *La poesía lírica de Juan de la Cueva* (Sevilla: Publicaciones de la Excma. Diputación Provincial de Sevilla, 1980), p. 58. "en miércoles veinte y tres días del mes de octubre, año de mil y quinientos y cuarenta y tres años, batizó [sic] francisco fernández de hervas, cura de esta yglesia, a juan, hijo del doctor martín núñez de la cueva y su mujer juana de las cuevas, su mujer legítima. fueron padrinos francisco román, fiscal de la santa ynquisición, y el beneficiado francisco benítez de zama, y juan de medina, administrador de las cinco llagas, y bartolomé de lascarras alcaide de triana-francisco fernández de hervas cleg." Hereafter Reyes Cano.

See also José María Reyes Cano, "Documentos relativos a Juan de la Cueva: Nuevos datos para su biografía," *Archivo Hispalense* 196 (1981), 107-35.

[4] The poem was printed in *Archivo Hispalense,* 1 (1886), 261-72, 290-309; 2 (1886), 17-24, 41-8, 65-72, 87-96.

[5] Wulff, p. xxxv. "Les enfants de Da Catalina, c'est-à-dire les cousins de Juan, étaient Andres Çamudio de Alfaro, médecin de Philippe II et de la 'general Inquisicion' . . . ."

Luciano de Negrón, son of a prosecuting attorney for the Council of Castile, who "achieved prominence in Seville as preacher, humanist and poet."[6] It thus appears that Juan was born into and nurtured by a family which counted among its members a royal physician, preachers, poets, and an Inquisitor. His apparent predisposition toward church and toward writing is not surprising in one born to an intellectual family in Spanish society of that time.

The atmosphere in sixteenth-century Seville had a profound effect upon Juan de la Cueva. The discovery of the New World brought wealth and importance to the city. The Casa de Contratación was established there to regulate trade between Spain and her colonies. The abundance and variety of the goods which flowed into the city benefitted the whole society.[7] This affluence contributed to the development of Seville's rich intellectual and artistic tradition. Juan de la Cueva had literary connections with such Sevillians as Juan de Mal Lara, Diego Girón, and Fernando de Herrera. He was acquainted with the Enríquez de Ribera family which held the titles of Marquis of Tarifa and Duke of Alcalá. The Enríquez de Ribera family was noted for its patronage of the arts and of a literary academy which met at the family home, the Casa de Pilatos. Academies, similar to salons of our day where amateur and professional artists, musicians, or authors meet to discuss, read, and perform their works, flourished throughout Seville.[8] The following post script added to the end of Cueva's "Epístola a Cristóbal de Sayas de Alfaro" indicates that Cueva participated in the city's vibrant cultural activities:

En Hispalis catorce de febrero del ano del Senor de ochenta y cinco a

---

Ruth Pike, *Aristocrats and Traders. Sevillian Society in the Sixteenth Century* (Ithaca: Cornell University Press, 1972), p. 86. "This (commission to write a book on the plague) occurred during the epidemic of 1568, when Doctors Andrés Zamudio de Alfaro and Francisco Franco were both asked to prepare treatises about the pestilence of that year." Hereafter Pike.

6 Pike, p. 61; "Another (canon of Genoese descent) was Dr. Luciano de Negrón (1562-1606), son of Licentiate Carlos de Negrón, prosecuting attorney for the Council of Castile. Dr. Negrón achieved prominence in Seville as a preacher, humanist and poet."

7 Antonio Domínguez Ortiz, *Orto y ocaso de Sevilla*, 3a. edición, Colección de bolsillo, número 31 (Sevilla: Universidad de Sevilla, 1981), p. 22. "Este cúmulo de novedades provocó una fermentación prodigiosa, una revolución sin precedentes en todos los órdenes de la vida, cuyas consecuencias se dejaron sentir, por supuesto, en Sevilla antes que en ninguna otra parte." Hereafer Domínguez Ortiz.

8 See Willard F. King, "The Academies and Seventeenth-Century Spanish Literature," *PMLA*, 75 (1960), 367-76.

los academistas remitida del Museo del inclito Malara. Presente el Ilustrisimo de Gelves.[9]

We do not know whether Cueva married. He dedicated many Petrarchan-style love poems to Felipa de la Paz, whom he called Felicia. Wulff believes that Cueva met the woman in 1567 when he was about sixteen years old, and that his infatuation lasted about ten years.[10]

Lack of precise information about periods in Cueva life frustrates the researcher. One time period, however, is fairly certain. Cueva traveled to New Spain between 1574-1577 with his younger brother, Claudio, who for a time served the church in Guadalajara.[11] Before Juan returned to Spain in 1577, there was compiled an anthology of works of some thirty poets residing in Mexico entitled *Flores de baria poesía.*[12] Cueva's inclusion in the collection marked his literary debut.

Cueva returned in 1577 to Seville where he lived for all save the last two years of his life, and those he spent in Cuenca. Cueva participated in the intellectual and cultural life of his native city, wrote lyric and narrative poetry and verse dramas, produced his plays, and published an anthology containing 134 poems and another which contained his fourteen plays. Wulff believed that Cueva died around 1610.[13] José Reyes Cano, who discovered

---

[9] This *epístola* is found in MS 4.116 in the Biblioteca Nacional, Madrid. Also see Juan Montero, "Otro ataque contra las anotaciones herrerianas: La epístola 'A Cristóbal de Sayas de Alfaro' de Juan de la Cueva," *Revista de literatura,* 48, 95 (1986), pp. 19-33.

[10] Glenn, pp. 19-21; Wulff, p. xlv.

[11] Glenn, p. 20. "The summer of 1574, Cueva sailed from Seville for Mexico. Accompanying him was his younger brother Claudio, who had recently been ordained in anticipation of an ecclesiastic career. The precise motive for Juan's journey has never been established. His brother was traveling to Guadalajara to assume the post of Archdeacon. Juan doubtless remained in his brother's company until the decision to return to Seville was made in 1577."

Also see José Cebrián García, "Nuevos datos para las biografías del inquisidor Claudio de la Cueva (1551?-1611) y del poeta Juan de la Cueva (1543-1612) I," *Archivo Hispalense,* 202 (1983), 3-29.

[12] For further reference to the *Flores,* see Renato Rosaldo, "Flores de baria poesía. Apuntes preliminares para el estudio de un cancionero manuscrito mexicano del XVI," *Hispania,* 34 (1951), 177-80 and "Flores de baria poesía. Estudio preliminar de un cancionero inédito mexicano de 1577," *Abside,* 15, No. 3 (julio-sept., 1951), 373-96; No. 4 (oct.-dic., 1951), 523-50; 16, No. 1 (enero-marzo, 1952), 91-122.

[13] Wulff, p. xxxvii-xxxviii; ". . . en effect, depuis le 30 nov. 1606, où il termine et dédie, à Séville, son *Exemplar Poetico* (sic) au fils de son mécène, Fernando Enriquez de Ribera, je ne connais plus rien de sa main qui ne soit composé à Cuenca, où il

Cueva's baptismal certificate, also found Cueva's will which shows that he died in Granada in 1612.[14]

In the fifteenth, sixteenth, and seventeenth centuries the Church of Rome was an inseparable part of Spanish government as well as the daily life of families and individuals. The Catholic rulers, Ferdinand and Isabella, in their effort to unify Spain under a single monarchy and a single religion, petitioned Pope Sixtus IV to create in Spain a Holy Office of the Inquisition which would be under their direct control.[15] The Inquisition was an ecclesiastical tribunal whose duty it was to protect the faith from any heresies which might take root in Spain. The heresy which the Catholic Monarchs most feared came from Jews who had purportedly converted to Catholicism but in reality had not. Many of these *conversos*, as the Jewish converts were called, had for economic and social reasons declared themselves to be Christians but continued to practice Judaism in secret. Other Jews, on the other hand, accepted Christianity and became high-ranking officials in the government and in the church.

In October of 1480, two years after the pope had created the Spanish Inquisition, a tribunal was established in Seville to root out those *conversos* yet practicing their old faith. Barely three months had passed when the Sevillian tribunal staged its first *auto de fe*. The "act of faith" was a religious service in which the errant believers were restored to the fold of the faithful. If the *converso* did not recant, he was "relaxed" to the secular arm of the Inquisition to be burnt as a heretic.

Conversos, or New Christians, continued to be suspect well into the seventeenth-century. Spanish society as a whole became so fearful of persecution that people felt compelled to authenticate their credentials as "Old Christians" and to establish that their heritage contained no taint of Jewish blood.

In the early years of the sixteenth century, the threat of the Protestant Reformation, especially the protest of Martin Luther, caused the Spanish Inquisition to take strong measures to prevent the infiltration of the Reforma-

---

a souscrit (?), en 1609, une copie de l'*Exemplar.* Cette date est la dernière que nous ayons de sa vie."

[14] Reyes Cano, p. 58n46. "No obstante, dada la cantidad y la importancia de los datos que contiene sobre el poeta y su familia iremos adelantando algunos, ya que incluye el testamento del propio Cueva, quien murió en Granada, en 1.612, y no en Cuenca en 1.609 como se ha venido diciendo. Me referiré a él por 'Documento inédito I'."

[15] Henry Kamen, *The Spanish Inquisition* (New York: The New American Library, 1965). Hereafter Kamen.

tion into Spanish life. The *auto de fe* now served as an effective method of eliminating Protestantism in Spain. Again, the zeal of the Sevillian tribunal rid that city of any form of heresy. The second burning of Protestants in Spain occurred in Seville in September of 1559, four months after a similar event in the northern city of Valladolid.[16] Protestantism never became a real threat in Spain, because, from the first, Spaniards were taught it was a "sinister threat to their country and a direct blasphemy of God,"[17] and they dealt with it promptly and sternly.

Juan de la Cueva's family appears to have been Old Christian and fiercely loyal to the Roman Catholic Church. Many of the family members took holy orders. His brother Claudio was Archdeacon in Guadalajara, Mexico, and later an Inquisitor in Spain. Cueva writes that his brother and his cousin, Luciano de Negrón, were active participants in the Spanish struggle against the Lutheran heresy.[18]

It is inescapable that this religious environment influenced Cueva as a man and as a writer. Living in the shadow of the Cathedral and its renowned bell tower, la Giralda, the dominant architectural feature in Seville then (and now), he could scarcely have avoided a strong religious bent. This was reinforced by his family's devotion to the church. Cueva's writings clearly reflect his devout bias, and that influence upon *Comedia de la libertad de España por Bernardo del Carpio* will be discussed hereinafter.

The selection of such historical subjects as Bernardo del Carpio and the Infantes de Lara was, at that time, a novelty in the Spanish theater. Thereto-

---

[16] Kamen, p. 79-80. "Yet once again well-meaning men were prey to the tensions gripping Europe, and the result was a series of *autos de fe* which burnt out Protestantism in Spain. The first holocaust was held at Valladolid on Trinity Sunday, 29th May 1559. . . . It was now the turn of Seville. The first great *auto* there was held on Sunday, 24 September 1559."

[17] Kamen, p. 81.

[18] Juan de la Cueva, *Historia y sucesión de la Cueva,* in *Archivo Hispalense,* 2 (1886). In strophe LV (p. 69), he writes of his brother Claudio: "que el impero/tendrá en punir la cisma de Lutero." In strophe LXV (p. 72),

> Contra el rebelde Apóstata, que huye
> la verdadera ley, que el verdadero
> legislador dió al mundo, que destruye
> la cisma, y pertinacia de Lutero
> calificando el ciego error, que argulle
> LUCIANO DE NEGRON, de quien espera
> un puesto insigne que sea en el mundo,
> el que no tiene fuera de él segundo.

fore, the drama had consisted of representations of scenes from the liturgical year, farces in which shepherds fell in and out of love, and realistic depictions of everyday life. That was the genre that characterized the work of Cueva's predecessor playwrights such as Juan del Encina, Lucas Fernández, Bartolomé de Torres Naharro, and Lope de Rueda. Cueva's unprecedented dramatization from Spanish history was followed some twenty years later by Lope de Vega. Historical plays such as Lope de Vega's *Fuenteovejuna* and *El bastardo Mudarra*, Guillén de Castro's *Las mocedades del Cid*, and Tirso de Molina's *Los amantes de Teruel* were the result of a trend which began with Juan de la Cueva's theater.

In addition to his plays, Juan de la Cueva produced a wide variety of both lyric and narrative poetry. Among his short lyrical works were at least 226 sonnets, twenty-five *elegías*, twenty-one *canciones*, eighteen *epístolas*, seven eclogues, two madrigals and one *sestina*.[19] Few of these have ever been published.[20] The cataloguing, by Battle and by Glenn does not list the poems written by Cueva and included in the unpublished *Flores de baria poesía*.

The longer poems, mainly narrative in nature, have fared little better as regards their availability. They will be considered chronologically according to composition or manuscript date. The *Viage de Sannio* (1585), composed of 494 *octavas reales* divided into five books, recounts the journey of the buffoon, Sannio, to the throne of Jupiter where he expects recognition and reward for his literary efforts.[21] The *Viage* was first published in 1886.[22] The *Coro febeo de romances historiales* (1588) contains one hundred *romances* divided into ten books. Book I contains a dedication to Apollo; each of the succeeding nine is dedicated to one of the nine muses.[23] No modern edition

---

[19] John W. Battle, "Dramatic Unity in the Plays of Juan de la Cueva," Diss. Duke University 1970, pp. 181-90. Hereafter Battle.

[20] Bartolomé José Gallardo, *Ensayo de una biblioteca de libros raros y curiosos*, vol. 2 (Madrid: Imprenta y Estereotipia de M. Rivadeneyra, 1863), pp. 637-736.

Agustín Durán, ed., *Romancero general o Colección de romances castellanos anteriores al siglo XVIII*, Biblioteca de Autores Españoles, 10 & 16 (Madrid: Atlas, 1945).

Juan Joseph López de Sedano, ed., *Parnaso español. Colección de poesías escogidas de los más célebres poetas castellanos*, vols. 4, 8, & 9 (Madrid: Antonio de Sancha, 1770-1778).

[21] Glenn, pp. 138-44.

[22] Wulff, pp. 1-62.

[23] Antonio Rodríguez-Moñino, *Manual bibliográfico de cancioneros y romanceros* (Madrid: Editorial Castalia, 1973), vol. 1, pp. 9-17.

has been published. *La conquista de la Bética,* written and published in 1603, and reprinted in 1795,[24] is an epic which narrates the Spanish Reconquest of Seville by King Ferdinand III and contains more than ten thousand *octavas reales* divided into twenty-four cantos.

Two mythological poems are *El llanto de Venus en la muerte de Adonis* and *Los amores de Marte i Venus,* both written in *octavas reales.* The *Llanto* was included in the only anthology of his poems that was printed during Cueva's lifetime. That version of the poem is made up of seventy- eight *octavas.* Later, in 1604, Cueva expanded the *Llanto* by adding some fifty strophes. This expansion was published in a *festschrift* in 1962.[25] Next appeared the *Historia y sucesión de la Cueva* in 1604, as mentioned earlier. *Los inventores de las cosas* (1607) is a "treatise in blank verse divided into four books" modeled on Polydorus Virgilius' (d. 1555) *De rerum inventoribus.*[26] The *Inventores* remained in manuscript until 1778 when Juan Joseph López de Sedano published it in his *Parnaso español.* A modern critical edition appeared in 1980.[27] Two undated works, *La muracinda* and *La batalla entre ranas i ratones,* survive only as manuscript fragments.[28] Cueva's translation of the *Officina de Juan Ravisio Textor,* which describes "the pedigrees of the pagan gods and their cults," has been missing since 1844.[29]

Near the end of his productive life, reflecting upon his own writing and that of the Italian and Spanish poets, Cueva wrote the *Exemplar poético.* Penned in 1608 and recopied and corrected in 1609, it is the most readily available of his works.[30] Written in tercets in three epistles, the work recommends stylistic rules for poetic composition. He prescribed use of writing style

---

24 Battle, pp. 198-201.

25 Paul Verdevoye, "Le poème 'Llanto de Venus en la muerte de Adonis, de Juan de la Cueva dans sa version définitive en partie inédite" in *Mélanges offerts a Marcel Bataillon par les hispanistes françois, Bulletin Hispanique,* 64 bis (1962), 677-89. See also José Cebrián García, ed. *Juan de la Cueva. Fábulas mitológicas y épica burlesca.* Madrid: Editora Nacional, 1984 and *La fábula de Marte y Venus de Juan de la Cueva. Significación y sentido.* Sevilla: Publicaciones de la Universidad de Sevilla 1986.

26 Glenn, pp. 144-45.

27 Beno Weiss and Louis C. Pérez, *Juan de la Cueva's Los Inventores de las Cosas* (University Park, Pa.: Pennsylvania State University Press, 1980).

28 Battle, p. 203. Glenn, p. 147. Also see José Cebrián García, "Juan de la Cueva, Traductor de la (Batracomiomaquia)," *Revista de literatura,* 47, 93 (1985), pp. 23-39.

29 Glenn, p. 147. Also Battle, pp. 189-90.

30 Icaza, p. xxvii. ". . . éste fechado en Sevilla en 1606 y corregido en 1609, última noticia de la vida de Cueva ..."

to convey accurately and graphically the action or mood which the poet had selected. That is, words and accents appropriate to such action or mood should be used. For example, he said, to convey magnificent heroism one should use fierce-sounding words and to convey grief, gentle and sad words. One should not mix the wrath of Mars with the gentleness of love. He insisted that the poet choose only subjects which were consistent with his views and never attempt to write about that which was repugnant to conscience or to literary taste.

While devoting relatively little space to drama, Cueva in *Exemplar poético* writes a defense of the Spanish national theater with some advice for the would-be playwright.[31] He reminds his reader that in the evolving dramatic form he introduced kings and gods to the stage, changed the number of acts from five to four, and called the divisions *jornadas*. He suggests that Spanish dramatists disregard the classical unities of time and place. He suggests use of stereotyped characters; and he advocates that poetry be written in style and verse appropriate to the speaker and to the occasion (III, 640-641). He adds that the dramatist must not forget that his purpose is to entertain.

Cueva's dramatic works, the *Comedias y tragedias*, have fortunately fared better than his poetry as regards their accessibility. Fourteen plays survive.[32] These were initially published in 1583 as a dramatic anthology. The sole surviving copy of the *princeps* was discovered at the Nationalbibliothek in Vienna by Adalbert Hämel in 1910.[33] The *princeps* has not been reedited nor republished since its appearance. The second edition containing fourteen plays is dated 1588. That edition has notes which state that the plays were performed in Seville from 1579 through 1581. It also contains *argumentos* for each play and for each act.

The first play in the collection, *Comedia de la muerte del rey don Sancho y reto de Çamora por don Diego Ordóñez,* treats of the epic theme of the death of Sancho II at the hands of Vellido Dolfos and the freeing of Zamora from Sancho's siege. The second play, *Comedia del saco de Roma y muerte*

---

[31] Icaza, pp. 161-69, lines 478-757.

[32] See Francisco Rodríguez Marín, *Nuevos datos para las biografías de cien escritores de los siglos XVI y XVII* (Madrid: Tipografía de la Revista de Archivos, Bibliotecas y Museos, 1923), p. 514. Marín published a document which shows that Cueva sought to publish a *segunda parte* of his plays in 1595. We do not know whether Cueva completed the project for no copies are known to exist.

[33] Adalbert Hämel, *Der Cid im spanischen Drama des XVI und XVII Jahrhunderts* (Halle: n.p., 1910). Hämel also published his findings in Spanish in an article, "Sobre la primera edición de las obras dramáticas de Juan de la Cueva," *Revista de Filología Española*, 10 (1923), 182-83.

de Borbón y coronación de nuestro invicto emperador Carlos Quinto, deals with events surrounding the Sack of Rome in 1527 by the Spanish and German Imperial troops of the Holy Roman Empire under the leadership of the Emperor's general, the Duke of Bourbon. The third, *Tragedia de los siete Infantes de Lara,* treats of the revenge of Gonzalo Bustos, through his bastard son Mudarra, upon Ruy Velásquez and Doña Llambra who caused the deaths of Bustos' seven legitimate sons. The fourth play, *Comedia de la libertad de España por Bernardo del Carpio*, the subject of this study, concerns the routing of the French under Charlemagne from Spanish soil by Bernardo del Carpio. *Comedia del degollado,* the fifth play, is a complex love intrigue involving Christians and Moors.

In the *Tragedia de la muerte de Ayax Telemón sobre las armas de Aquiles,* the sixth play, Cueva turns to the period of the Trojan War for inspiration. The seventh play, *Comedia del tutor*, deals with love of a student for a young girl and the ensuing complications when his guardian and a fellow student try to woo her. *Comedia de la constancia de Arcelina*, the eighth play, concerns a lady who saves her lover from execution by confessing to a murder which she herself has committed but for which he has assumed the blame. The ninth play, *Tragedia de la muerte de Virginia y Appio Claudio*, found thematic inspiration in Roman history. The play revolves around the lust of the Roman official, Appius Claudius for the virtuous Virginia who spurns his advances. When Appius invents lies about her, Virginia is brought to trial, whereupon her father appears and stabs her. Claudius in turn is sentenced to death.

The tenth and eleventh plays, *Comedia del príncipe tirano* and *Tragedia del príncipe tirano* seem to form a unit.[34] The plays focus on the rise of a prince to his father's throne and his subsequent fall from the throne, detailing the deceit and cruelty he uses to obtain his ends. *Comedia del viejo enamorado*, the twelfth play, portrays the schemes of an old man to steal the love of a young girl from her beloved. Romance, however, prevails when the old man dies and the true lovers are united. Cueva looked once more to ancient Rome for the subject of his thirteenth play, *Comedia de la libertad de Roma por Mucio Cévola.* As a main theme for this drama Cueva chose the expulsion of the Tarquinii from Rome and the liberation of that city from Etruscan

---

[34] Glenn, p. 97. "These two dramas with the same title — one a comedy and the other a tragedy — form one long play, the second being a sequel to the first. They were, in all probability, performed at the same time — in the Huerta de Doña Elvira in 1580. Cueva earns for himself with these plays the distinction of being the first Spanish playwright to compose a two-part drama."

control. The familiar plot of Cueva's fourteenth drama, *Comedia del infamador*, deals with the ineffectual attempts of Leucino to gain Eliodora's love. His slander causes her to be jailed. Through the intervention of the goddess Diana, however, Leucino then dies an ignoble death. This play and *Tragedia de los siete Infantes de Lara* are Cueva's best known plays.

As with his poetry, editions of Cueva's dramas are unfortunately very limited. The one edition which has been most readily available is that of Icaza in Clásicos castellanos (volume 60) which contains the *Exemplar poético, El infamador,* and *Los siete Infantes de Lara.* The first modern printing of the *Comedias y tragedias* was made by the same Icaza in 1917 for the Sociedad de Bibliófilos Españoles. Icaza based that printing on the second edition (1588) of the plays. Scholars have republished with commentaries only the *Infantes de Lara* and the *Infamador.*

In 1974, Anthony Watson published *Comedia de la libertad de España por Bernardo del Carpio* in the Exeter Hispanic Texts series.[35] In that publication he compared the language of that play as found in the 1583 *princeps,* with the language found in the three extant copies of the 1588 edition, and with that found in Icaza's 1917 printing of the 1588 version, making many cogent commentaries.

In order to edify or persuade as well as to entertain, Juan de la Cueva needed a subject for his fourth play in which he could espouse his moral and religious principles and his political and patriotic viewpoints. The formula required a strong legendary hero imbedded in the history and romance of his native Spain. Cueva turned to the Spanish Middle Ages and found in the medieval legend of Bernardo del Carpio the necessary ingredients he was seeking.

[35] Juan de la Cueva, *La libertad de España por Bernardo del Carpio*, ed. Anthony Watson, Exeter Hispanic Texts, No. 8 (Exeter: University Printing Unit, 1974).

Chapter II
In Search of the Historical Bernardo

Patriotism, liberty, and love of family set the tone of the Spanish medieval legend of Bernardo del Carpio. Bernardo, so the story goes, killed Roland, the bravest of Charlemagne's twelve Peers, during the battle of Roncesvalles. While that event was the Spanish hero's most famous exploit, Bernardo was revered for the love and tenacity with which for the rest of his life he sought the release of his father from a long, unjust imprisonment. Beginning as early as the thirteenth century, Spanish historians, and poets, joined later by the dramatists, included some form of the legend of Bernardo del Carpio in their works.

The Tradition of Bernardo del Carpio in the Latin and Spanish Chronicles: 1236-1541[1]

There is not a single traditional story of Bernardo del Carpio, but rather several, and they are not always parallel. Frustration inescapably attends one's efforts to weave the strands of the Bernardo legend into a meaningful, cohesive story, as the result of differences which abound in the two early

---

[1] A standard of spelling of character names which vary from chronicle to chronicle has been used. The *Primera crónica general* contains the majority of the variants. For San Diaz Sancho is used; for Bernaldo, Bernardo; for Tiobalte, Tibalte. Cueva prefers Alonso over Alfonso and Carlo Mano over Carlo Magno. Cueva's spelling will be followed when discussing the play.

chronicles, Lucas de Tuy's *Chronicon mundi* (1236) and Rodrigo Ximénez de Rada's *De rebus Hispaniae* (1243). The difficulty, however, does not stop there. Alfonso X, in the *Primera crónica general* (1270s), pointed out that the chronicles, as well as ballads and epic poetry, recorded different events in the life of Bernardo and in some instances described the same event in divergent ways. He made no attempt to reconcile these differences, but we are indebted to him for preservation of ancient history and tradition in its rich diversity.[2] We are also indebted to the scholarship of Florián de Ocampo for uncovering additional events in Bernardo's life, and these he added to an edition of Alfonso's *Primera crónica general* which he edited and published in 1541.[3]

The earliest written documentation of the Bernardo tradition is contained in Lucas de Tuy's *Chronicon mundi* written in Latin around the year 1236.[4] Lucas, who was Bishop of Tuy, discusses the reign of Alfonso II, King of Asturias and León, who was called "The Chaste," in Book IV. He records that Ximena, Alfonso's sister, and Count Sancho produced out of wedlock a son whom they named Bernardo. When the king learned of their

---

[2] For a discussion of the origins of the legend see the following works:

Manuel Milá y Fontanals, *De la poesía heroico-popular castellana* (Barcelona: Librería de Alvaro Verdaguer, 1874), pp. 130-72.

Marcelino Menéndez y Pelayo, "*Las mocedades de Bernardo del Carpio*," in *Estudios sobre el teatro de Lope de Vega*, in *Edición nacional de las obras completas de Menéndez Pelayo*, vol. 31 (Madrid: Consejo Superior de Investigaciones Científicas, 1949) pp. 122-214.

Albert B. Franklin III, "A Study of the Origins of the Legend of Bernardo del Carpio," *Hispanic Review*, 5 (1937), 286-303.

Albert B. Franklin III, "The Origin of the Legend of Bernardo del Carpio," Diss. Harvard 1938.

[3] To avoid confusion, a standard spelling of Ocampo's name has been used throughout the chapter. In the 1541 edition his name appears as "Docampo."

[4] The Latin text of Lucas de Tuy's history as well as the Latin text of Ximénez de Rada's chronicle has been used exclusively. Because an edition of Lucas de Tuy's history in Latin is extremely rare, Theodor Heinermann's *Untersuchungen zur Entstehung der Sage von Bernardo del Carpio* (Halle: Max Niemeyer, 1927) provides the researcher with the appropriate text. Heinermann further accommodates the researcher by printing the texts of Lucas de Tuy, of Ximénez de Rada, and of the *PCG* side-by-side so that comparisons may be made quickly. Marcelino Menéndez y Pelayo also printed Lucas de Tuy's text in his study of Lope de Vega's *Las mocedades de Bernardo del Carpio* (see note 2 above). An early fourteenth-century translation into Spanish of *Chronicon mundi* proved helpful, although certain minor discrepancies appear in the translation from Latin to Spanish. For that translation, see Lucas, Obispo de Tuy, *Crónica de España*, ed. Julio Puyol (Madrid: Tipografía de la Revista de Archivos, Bibliotecas y Museos, 1926).

affair, he became infuriated and imprisoned the count in the castle of Luna in the province of León.[5] In addition, King Alfonso sent his erring sister to live out her days in a convent. Having no son of his own, Alfonso reared Bernardo with affection at the palace. Bernardo grew to be a young man "statura magnus, vultu decorus, suauis eloquio, ingenio clarus, armis strenuus, et consilio prouidus" (Heinermann, p. 5).

Lucas de Tuy then tells that Charlemagne, King of France and Holy Roman Emperor, was fighting Arabs ("Sarracenos") in southwestern France when he crossed the Pyrenees and added to his empire "Gotthos et Hispanos qui erant in Catalonia et in montibus Vasconiae et in Nauarra" (Heinermann, p. 6). When he was in Spain, Charlemagne wrote to Alfonso, ordering him to become his subject and vassal ("subditus et vasallus"). When Bernardo obtained possession of the letters, he became angry, and joined with Spanish Moors to fight against Charlemagne.

Charlemagne captured the cities of Tudela, Nájera, and Monte Jardín. Satisfied with his victories, he decided to return to France. Bernardo, however, in league with Marsil, the Moorish King of Zaragoza, and with a band of Navarrese soldiers, pursued Charlemagne. Those combined forces attacked and defeated the rearguard of the French army. Among the fallen enemy was Roland, the bravest and most famous of the Twelve Peers of France, Charlemagne's elite band of knights.

Later, the Emperor put together another army and vindicated the defeat at Roncesvalles with a great victory over the Moors.[6] He made a pilgrimage to Santiago de Compostela to give thanks to God for the victory. Soon thereafter Charlemagne made peace with Alfonso, and through Alfonso he met Bernardo. Charlemagne persuaded Bernardo to return with him to Aachen, where the young Spaniard made many friends.

Bernardo appears once more in Lucas de Tuy's history.[7] During the reign of Alfonso III, Bernardo was again in Spain fighting alongside the king against the Moors, Bernardo's erstwhile allies. Bernardo made the castle of Carpio in Salamanca his residence, and from that time he was known as Ber-

---

[5] *Enciclopedia Universal Ilustrada* (Madrid: Espasa-Calpe, 1907?-30), vol. 31, p. 795.

[6] Lucas de Tuy does not indicate whether Charlemagne returned to France before he made his second assault on Spain nor where the second battle took place. The *Primera crónica general* states that Charlemagne "quando el allego Alemannia, desbaratado de la batalla, que se aquiso et se apodero et dio tornada a Çaragoça, et cerco y el rey Marsil." (Heinermann, p. 12).

[7] Ramiro I and Ordoño I ruled between Alfonso II and Alfonso III. None of the historians include a reference to Bernardo during the interim reigns.

nardo del Carpio. About that time Bernardo learned that Alfonso II had cast his natural father, Count Sancho, into prison. The hero was ready to rebel against his king, but Alfonso III promised to free Sancho if Bernardo would help in fighting the Moors. Bernardo agreed, and he and the king fought together in many battles. Lucas de Tuy's final mention of Bernardo concerns the hero's death.[8] "Eo tempore mortuus est Bernaldus fortissimus miles" (Heinermann, p. 27).

Rodrigo Ximénez de Rada, following the work of Lucas de Tuy and also writing in Latin, relates the Bernardo legend in his work, *De rebus Hispaniae* (1243), Book IV, Chapters 9, 10, 15, and 16.[9] The story is essentially the same but with certain important differences. The first is that Bernardo's parents, Ximena and Sancho, had been married secretly, a point retained in later chronicles. This is a critical distinction, because if Bernardo were indeed legitimate, his social and legal positions are changed significantly. He could be considered an appropriate successor to the throne. And the sequestration of his parents by the king was unjustified. Bernardo's life-long effort to free his father assumes a more important dimension.

The second difference in Ximénez de Rada's narration is that Alfonso, tired from a long reign but having no son to succeed him, sent a secret messenger to Charlemagne. Alfonso promised that he would relinquish the Spanish throne to the Emperor if he would send military aid to help fight the Moors in Spain. Charlemagne responded that he would help when he finished his own campaign against Arabic invasions into France. When the messenger returned to Spain, Bernardo and the privy council learned of Alfonso's secret invitation to the French. They demanded that the king revoke the pact or be expelled from Spain. Alfonso rescinded his promise, and this action caused Charlemagne to become angry and to send troops into Spain.

Another addition to the legend tells of Christians living in the Pyrenees whose liberty was threatened by Charlemagne's invading forces. Those peo-

---

8 Lucas de Tuy does not record the place nor the cause of Bernardo's death. Presumably it occurred at Carpio as a result of natural causes.

9 Rodrigo Ximénez de Rada, *De rebus Hispaniae* as it is found in Elio Antonio de Nebrija, Habes in hoc volvmine amice lector. Aelii Antonii Nebrissensis Rervm a Fernando & Elisabe Hispaniarum foelicissimis Regibus gestar Decades duae. Necnon belli Nauariensis libros duos. Annexa insuper Archiepiscopi Roderici Chronica, aliisque historiis antehac non excussis. (Granatam: [Xanthos Nebrisenses], 1545). The Archbishop's history is the third of six histories contained in this volume. The first two histories, written by Nebrija, are printed on folios i-lxxvi. New pagination begins with the Archbishop's history, folios i-lxxxiiii. Hereafter, Ximénez de Rada.

ple vowed to fight rather than lose their freedom. To the casual reader, that brief comment might seem unimportant to the legend, since it does not affect the outcome of the story. It does, however, make a positive statement about the Spanish people and their love of freedom. Independence from a foreign power has played a significant role throughout Spanish history.

Ximénez de Rada's narration of the battle of Roncesvalles significantly differs from earlier versions. He relates that part of the French army remained at the foot of the Pyrenees while a vanguard, under the leadership of Roland, ascended to a high elevation. In this narration it is Alfonso rather than Bernardo who led the Spanish attack which annihilated the cream of the French army. Charlemagne, who was with his forces in another sector, arrived at the scene too late to help. He then fled to Germany to plan another attack on Spain, but he died before that plan could be executed. Ximénez de Rada concludes his narration of the Bernardo legend as Alfonso III, true to his promise, granted a pardon to Sancho.[10]

Alfonso X, The Wise, greatly expands the account of Bernardo's life in the *Primera crónica general* (1270s) by including Bernardo's adventures which had been passed through the oral tradition.[11] In addition the writer of this third version, for the first time in Spanish historiography, utilizes monologue and dialogue as a part of the narration and calculates dates according to the calendar of the Hispanic Era.

The first significant event is that Alfonso II sent two nobles, Orios Godos and Tibalte, to Saldaña as escorts to bring Sancho to the court at León. Meanwhile, Alfonso secretly ordered the arrest of Sancho to be carried out upon the count's arrival at court, and his orders were dutifully executed. Such harsh methods were used by the king's men that when they bound the count's wrists, "le fizieron salir la sangre por las vnnas" (*PCG*, v. 2, 352). The reader receives an insight into the monarch's cruelty when he states that such treatment is deserved "asaz mereçiestes et feziestes todo de como vos auino con donna Ximena." (*PCG*, v. 2, 352). Notwithstanding, Sancho asked that Alfonso personally rear his son Bernardo, who was then being brought up in another part of the kingdom.

---

[10] Ximénez de Rada does not record whether Sancho was released from his imprisonment after the pardon. Neither does he record Bernardo's death.

[11] Alfonso X, el Sabio, *Primera crónica general de España*, ed. Ramón Menéndez Pidal, 2 vols. (Madrid: Editorial Gredos, 1955). Hereafter *PCG*. Menéndez Pidal writes on page XLV in vol 1: "Sus prosificaciones y resúmenes constituyen una inestimable recopilación de los principales textos épicos de entonces, hecha con autoridad regia una especie de codificación oficial de la epopeya."

The writer of the *PCG* includes a new episode in the story. Two relatives of Bernardo, Blasco Meléndez and Suero Velásquez, were worried about Sancho. Because they were sworn to silence by Alfonso concerning Sancho's fate, the two were intent upon finding a means of revealing the truth to Bernardo about his natural father and his whereabouts. The men devised a plan in which they approached two kinswomen of Bernardo, María Meléndez and Urraca Sánchez, whose collaboration could help them accomplish their purpose. The two women were to challenge Bernardo to a chess game and permit him to win. Then they must inform him who his parents were and tell him that his father was languishing in prison. The plan succeeded. Bernardo dressed in mourning, and when Alfonso asked the reason for his grief, Bernardo was afforded the opportunity to plead his father's cause. Alfonso's response was brief and strong:

> partitme vos delante, et nunca jamas seades osado de dezirme esto, ca yo vos prometo que nunca veredes vuestro padre, nin saldra de las torres mientre yo uiua.
>
> (*PCG*, v. 2, 355)

Bernardo countered that he would continue to plead for his father's freedom and continue to serve his king faithfully. The remaining account of Bernardo's history, contained in Chapters 649-656 of the *PCG*, does not form a part of Cueva's plot and need not be pursued.

Bernardo receives further treatment in Florián de Ocampo's *Crónica de España* (1541), an edition of Alfonso X's *Primera crónica general.*[12] The hero appears in the narration of the reigns of Alfonso II, The Chaste (tercera parte, folios ccxxiii-ccxxxi) and Alfonso III, The Great (tercera parte, folios ccxxxv-ccxxxviii). Ocampo's treatment of the secret marriage of Ximena and Sancho and the latter's imprisonment is substantially the same as that of the *PCG*, although the narrator makes no mention of the gory detail of the tight fetters.

Ocampo also tells of Alfonso's invitation to Charlemagne to assume the Spanish throne, of the grandees' ultimatum to Alfonso, and of Alfonso's revoking the invitation. The historian adds that Charlemagne responded to that revocation with a letter in which he demanded subjugation of the Spanish.

---

[12] Las quatro partes enteras de la Cronica de Espana que mando Componer el Serenissimo rey don Alfonso llamado el sabio, Uista y emendada mucha parte de su impresion por el maestro Florian Docampo. (Zamora: Agustin de Paz y Juan Picardo, 1541). Hereafter *CGE*.

Ocampo describes the plan of Suero and Blasco to use the two noblewomen, María and Urraca, as a means of revealing Bernardo's parentage. In the 1541 version of the story the women do not play chess, but simply inform the hero.

As with the *PCG,* Ocampo includes events in Bernardo's life which Cueva chose not to dramatize and which, therefore, are not relevant to this study.

The Tradition of Bernardo del Carpio in Spanish Ballads and Epics

Lucas de Tuy, Ximénez de Rada, the *PCG*, and the *CGE* mention frequently *cantares* and *fablas* which provide details about the legend of Bernardo del Carpio. By the mid-sixteenth century, *romances,* or ballads, which employed episodes from folklore, lives of the heroes, and national history as topics were very popular. Agustín Durán in the nineteenth century and Ramón Menéndez Pidal in this century collected ballads from many sources and assembled them into two collections which are readily accessible.[13] Each of those contains a section devoted to the *romancero* of Bernardo del Carpio. Altogether they contain more than seventy ballads.

The ballads were a means of entertaining and of transmitting both popular and national history from one generation to another. Many of the *romances* dealing with Bernardo narrate the same events found in the chronicles. Other ballads, such as "Con ansia estrema y lloroso" and "Cuando el padre Faetón," portray Bernardo as a courtly knight who saves maidens in distress. The poetic style of the ballads offers a freedom in the portrayal of character not afforded in the historical accounts. As a result, the poets capitalize upon certain moments in the hero's life as points of heightened interest. They uniformly sing of the strained relationship between King Alfonso and Bernardo which results from the king's unswerving denial to release the hero's father, Count Sancho. Other *romances* recount Bernardo's skirmishes with rival Christian and Moorish knights and the preparation for the aftermath of the battle of Roncesvalles without any description of the battle itself.

---

[13] *Romancero general,* ed. Agustín Durán, 2 vols. (Madrid: Atlas, 1945). Hereafter *RG*.

Romancero tradicional de las lenguas hispánicas, ed. Ramón Menéndez Pidal, 2 vols. (Madrid: Editorial Gredos, 1957).

The ballads emphasize two personality traits in Bernardo: one, an intense paternal loyalty based on a sense of justice; the other, a deep-rooted patriotism founded on his belief in freedom. The balladeers artistically interweave the two traits as exemplified in "Por las riberas de Arlanza." Bernardo's loyalty to his father is revealed in the following quotation. Bernardo, armed for battle, rides up to Alfonso and addresses him on the king's lack of justice:

—Bastardo me llaman, Rey,
Siendo hijo de tu hermana,
Y del noble Sancho Diaz;
Ese Conde de Saldaña:
Dicen que ha sido traidor,
Y mala mujer tu hermana.
Tú y los tuyos lo habeis dicho,
Que otro ninguno no osara:
Mas quien quiera que lo ha dicho
Miente por medio la barba;
Mi padre no fué traidor,
Ni mi madre mujer mala,
Porque cuando fuí engendrado
Ya mi madre era casada.
Pusiste á mi padre en hierros,
Y á mi madre en órden santa,
Y por que no herede yo
Quieres dar tu reino á Francia.
Morirán los castellanos
Antes de ver tal jornada:
Montañeses, y leoneses,
Y ese gente esturiana [sic],
Y ese rey de Zaragoza
Me prestará su compaña
Para salir contra Francia
Y darle cruda batalla;
Y si buena me saliere,
Será el bien de toda España;
Si mala, por la república
Moriré yo en la demanda.
Mi padre mando que sueltes

Pues me diste la palabra;
Si no, en campo, como quiera
Te será bien demandada.

(*RG*, I, 427)

Bernardo's deep-rooted sense of patriotism can be appreciated in the following portion of another ballad entitled "Retirado en su palacio." Bernardo enters the palace to tell Alfonso that he will fight the French

y dize: —Si el miedo torpe
haze tan bajos efectos,
como es bien que el mundo note,
en la sangre ilustre y clara,
si es bien que sangre se nombre,
de aquellos famosos godos
de quien tembló todo el orbe,
¿cómo á la parlera fama
quereis obligar pregone
vuestros valerosos hechos
sujetos á otras naciones?
Primero el rigor del cielo
ardientes rayos arroje
sobre la aflicta Castilla
que nombre de esclavo tome.
Eso no consentiré,
que aunque el mundo se trastorne,
no ha de ser, ó han de morir
a mis manos sus autores,
que muchas ay sin las mias
para este efecto concordes,
que es dulce la libertad,
y la esclavitud inorme.

(*RG*, I, 428)

Beyond the chronicle and *romances* which form the point of departure for Cueva's play, Cueva may have had at his disposal the epic tradition as well. A detailed discussion of any reliance upon an epic source is impossible, however, because no version of a true *cantar de gesta* dealing with Bernardo is known to have survived. Professor William J. Entwistle postulates the existence of a *cantar* and of an *estoria* from which the scribe-historians fashioned their accounts of Bernardo del Carpio in the chronicles.[14] Entwistle's chronology and plot consist of the basic events noted above. One epic which makes reference to Bernardo is the *Poema de Fernán González,* written around the middle of the thirteenth century.[15] In verses 126-143 Bernardo appears as the liberator of Spain at the battle of Roncesvalles in much the same fashion as the chronicles indicate.

Bernardo del Carpio had inspired patriotic pride in the Spanish people for about eight hundred years prior to Cueva's decision to write about him. In an age when the Spanish Empire was at its height, retelling of the medieval legend of Bernardo reinforced the ideals which the dramatist believed to have made Spain great. The nation was prospering and so were its literature and fine arts. It was appropriate, although startling for the day, for the dramatist to adapt for the stage folk history surrounding a legendary hero. This was one of Juan de la Cueva's contributions to the emerging national theater.

---

[14] William J. Entwistle, "The 'Cantar de Gesta' of Bernardo del Carpio," *MLR*, 23 (1928), 307-22, 432-52.

[15] *Poema de Fernán González,* ed. Alonso Zamora Vicente, Clásicos castellanos, 128 (Madrid: Espasa-Calpe, 1970), p. xi.

Chapter III
The Play — Its Plot and Construction

Juan de la Cueva gave a new dimension to the story of Bernardo del Carpio when he molded the chronicled events into a dramatic presentation. No longer were the happenings and the characters solely words on a page or pictures in the mind's eye. The men and women who stepped on to the stage at the theater of the Atarazanas in Seville in 1579 to perform *Comedia de la libertad de España por Bernardo del Carpio* brought the legend to life. The audience must have left the theater with a greater appreciation of a glorious event in Spain's history engendered by a legendary hero. They must also have gained an awareness tnat Cueva's dramatization created a new version of the familiar story of Bernardo.

Cueva embellished the basic story in several ways. He chose the events which best suited his purpose and reorganized them to achieve dramatic effects. He expanded the roles of the characters in the chronicle account and added new characters of his own invention. He wove those events and characters together with the thread of language, not the Spanish of the average Sevillian, but a stylized, rhetorical language meant to please aesthetically and to emphasize themes and ideas.

The Plot

The play takes place in northern Spain during the reign of Alonso II of

Asturias and León.[1] Alonso is called "The Chaste" because he leads a pietistic and celibate life. He seems to accept the deference so paid him by his subjects as no more than his due, and through his inflated self-esteem he has developed a fragile "honor" which his subjects would do well not to offend.

As the play begins, King Alonso believes that his honor has been compromised by the furtiveness of the secret marriage of his sister, Ximena, to Sancho Días, Count of Saldaña. The monarch sends his messenger, Count Tibalte, to escort Ximena to the royal palace. Meanwhile Ximena and her confidante, Oliva, converse in Ximena's residence. She tells Oliva about her dejected state brought on by her separation from Sancho. When Tibalte arrives with the summons, Ximena expresses surprise but obediently accompanies Tibalte. When his sister arrives, Alonso accuses her of treason and refuses to listen to her pleas for understanding and compassion. To avenge the imagined affront to his royal dignity, Alonso harshly banishes Ximena to live out her days in a convent. She asks her brother to grant one request, that he rear her young son Bernardo at the court in León, but the brutal Alonso makes no response.

Alonso next turns his vengeance upon Sancho Días. The monarch once more uses his trusted messenger Tibalte, sending him this time to Saldaña to summon Sancho to León. As Tibalte goes to carry out his orders, he is torn between fealty to the Crown and loyalty to his friend Sancho. Conscience requires that he warn Sancho of the king's fury, and he decides to do so. When he confronts his friend, however, self-interest intervenes, and he is rendered unable to carry out his high-minded plan to save Sancho. Sancho, anxious to learn the reason for the ruler's summons, proposes a swift return to the capital. When the two men appear before Alonso, he orders that Sancho be seized. Then he ruthlessly sentences Sancho to be blinded and to serve life imprisonment in a castle in Luna; and the first part of that hideous sentence is carried out on stage.

Having attended to Bernardo's real parents, Alonso turns his attention to the boy. He orders his courtiers to bring his young nephew to León, telling them that he will be reared as Alonso's son. Despite this apparent act of generosity, the king never accepts Bernardo as the legitimate heir to his throne, and Bernardo grows up understanding that he is the king's illegitimate son.

[1] To avoid confusion between the sources and the play, Cueva's spelling of the character names has been retained throughout the discussion of the play. For that reason Alfonso is spelled Alonso; Díaz, Días; Blasco, Velasco; Carlomagno, Carlo Mano.

Some years later, King Alonso decides that it is time to retire. He stubbornly refuses to name Bernardo to be his successor. Secretly, Alonso has sent a delegation to Carlo Mano, emperor of the French (thinly disguised Charlemagne who has been gobbling up large parts of Europe), offering the throne to him. Knowing of the ruler's complicity and being deeply concerned for the integrity of their native Castile, two noblemen, Suero Velásquez and Velasco Meléndez, consider how best to avoid the impending catastrophe. They determine that the nation's salvation would be best entrusted to Bernardo. They reason that first Bernardo must know that he is not the bastard son of Alonso, but the legitimate son of Sancho. They, however, may not so inform Bernardo, as they remain under an oath of secrecy to the king regarding Alonso's treatment of Ximena and Sancho. The grandees, kinsmen of Sancho, recognize that they can remain faithful to the oath and yet inform Bernardo of his true parentage if they enlist the aid of two nuns, also related to Bernardo. When Suero and Velasco approach the women, the nuns agree to help. Setting the stage, the noblemen tell Bernardo about the impending French take-over. The nuns then tell Bernardo that he is not the illegitimate son of Alonso but rather the legitimate son of Sancho and Ximena, and they inform him of what has befallen his parents.

Bernardo is at first furious, but upon reflection, he realizes that the monarch would likely be more receptive to cool logic than to heated diatribe. Forcing himself to be diplomatic, he approaches his uncle and attempts to persuade him that the people would suffer harsh oppression if the king handed over his throne to France. Bernardo successfully convinces Alonso to retract his promise given to Carlo Mano. A messenger is then dispatched to the French emperor with a letter, written by Bernardo, informing him that Alonso has changed his mind.

Only after succeeding in his primary mission does Bernardo have another audience with his uncle. Bernardo now feels free to entreat Alonso to release Sancho from prison. Alonso agrees to grant Bernardo's plea for his father. During the audience, the messenger returns from France to inform Alonso that when Carlo Mano received the letter, he became infuriated and marshaled his troops to march against Spain. Furthermore, the French are at that moment fast approaching the Spanish border. Alonso promptly bestows command of the Spanish army upon Bernardo. The young man gathers his troops and moves out to engage the enemy at Roncesvalles.

Preparing for combat, Carlo Mano urges his troops to strive for a French victory. When battle is joined, Bernardo positions himself in the thick of the fighting. He cuts down Reinalte quickly and then dispatches Ancelino, thus costing the French two of their senior officers. He then engages Roldán, Carlo Mano's most trusted commander, and Roldán disarms him. Roldán throws down his sword, and the opposing commanders fight their battle hand-to-hand. Bernardo overcomes his gentlemanly enemy and chokes the life out of him with his bare hands.

Defeated, Carlo Mano laments the loss of his best officers at Bernardo's hands. He retrieves the body of the fallen hero, Roldán, and flees to France. Upon the withdrawal of the French, Bernardo proclaims victory and calls upon future generations to sing the glories of Spain. Marte, the god of War, descends to crown Bernardo with laurel as the liberator of Spain.

Major Variances From History

Cueva used the historical legend of Bernardo as a framework upon which to craft his play. He, however, refused to be bound rigidly by the legend as he knew it. The use of a mythological Roman god exemplifies his exercise of dramatic license. Other instances of his literary independence are equally apparent; still others are more subtle.

Cueva presents one of the few grisly moments in the early Spanish theater when, near the end of Act II, Alonso orders the on-stage blinding of Sancho. In the *PCG* Sancho appears before Alonso, who orders the count's wrists bound. The monarch's henchmen tie the fetters so tightly that Sancho's wrists bleed. Thus, while the chronicled history contained some gory detail, it does not compare with Cueva's invented scene. The gross physical act of having Sancho blinded on stage, while serving as shock value, was utilized primarily as a graphic metaphor to point up Alonso's degeneracy.

Among the various episodes which Cueva used in the plot of his drama is the plan of the two grandees by which Bernardo might learn that he is not the illegitimate child of the king but rather his legitimate nephew. Although the dramatist preserves the essence of this event, he changes it significantly by seeking out nuns to inform Bernardo of his heritage, thus giving the event greater weight and dignity and setting the stage leading to the redemption of Alonso. This episode occurs in the histories at an undetermined time after the battle of Roncesvalles. It sparks many lyrical passages in the ballads in which Bernardo pleads with his uncle to relax his severe treatment of Sancho. Cueva charges the scene with importance, by placing it immediately after

Alonso decides that Bernardo will not inherit the Spanish throne and directly before the foreign invasion and the armed conflict which follows.

In the sources the women who carry out the noblemen's project are *fijas dalgo*. Cueva makes them nuns and places the episode at the physical and spiritual center of the *comedia*. The scenes which comprise the episode (ll. 763-1194) lie within the middle third of the 1873 lines in the play. Just as surely the aesthetic center of the play is found in these lines. Within the first 762 lines Cueva bombards the audience with the monarch's unjust actions — first against Ximena, then against Sancho, and finally against Bernardo and the nation itself. Then Cueva, through his characters, comments on these occurrences. It is at this point that one begins to discern the poetic center of the play. The dramatist compels the audience, both consciously and subconsciously, to make a series of contrasts moving from the expressed deeds to the metaphorical deeds of the characters. Cueva achieves this through the actions of Alonso and those of the four major participants in this segment of the plot (Suero, Velasco, Urraca, and Bernardo).

Cueva takes considerable liberty when he dramatizes the battle at Roncesvalles. He conceives it as an encounter planned, by both sides, to occur at a specific point, Roncesvalles. Unable to stage a battle with a "cast of thousands," Cueva shows three one-on-one duels in which Bernardo eliminates three Peers of France: Reinalte, Ancelino, and Roldán. Furthermore, he adds two scenes of anagnorisis in which first a French captain (ll. 1659-1666) and then Carlo Mano (ll. 1771-1809) confront the shocking truth: that Carlo Mano has invaded Spain to slake his thirst for power and that Heaven has caused the defeat to teach him and the French a lesson.

Cueva chose those elements from the legend of Bernardo del Carpio and fashioned them into a dramatic form appropriate to theatrical convention of the sixteenth century. The compositional techniques which he employed contributed to the theatricalization of the events. And the importance to future Spanish playwrights of this *comedia* rests in large measure in its innovative construction.

Writing Techniques

Juan de la Cueva was, at the same time, a conventional and an innovative writer, and one can trace both these characteristics in *Comedia de la libertad de España por Bernardo del Carpio*. This drama contains 1873 lines.

The number is consequential only when one recalls that a *comedia* of the seventeenth century contained from about 2400 lines (Lope de Vega's *Fuenteovejuna*) to almost 4000 lines (Tirso de Molina's *El vergonzoso en palacio*). Cueva did not construct plots, subplots, and contrapuntal intrigue to the degree developed by his successors in the Spanish theater.

Juan de la Cueva, always the poet, wrote exclusively in verse. His language is at all times poetic. In *Comedia de la libertad de España por Bernardo del Carpio* the language is also highly rhetorical. In some instances the reader is struck by a turn of phrase that seems more in keeping with the seventeenth than with the sixteenth century. One must not forget that Cueva was a Sevillian poet, writing in a style that was favored by such poets as Fernando de Herrera and Luis de Góngora. Among the characteristics of that style were the use of rhetorical, ornate language and the favoring of Italianate meters, such as the octave and the tercet, over Spanish meters, such as the *romance*.

Rhetorical and poetic devices form an integral part of Cueva's dramatization of the legend of Bernardo del Carpio. Some of the devices simply give rhythm to the poetic line. Others are used for advocacy, whether it be for one character to persuade another, or for the playwright to sway the audience.[2]

Cueva was inventive when he wrote his play in polymetrical verse. Earlier dramatists had preferred to use prose or a single verse form. Cueva's varied use of stanzaic forms set a precedent for the Spanish theater of the seventeenth century in which polymetrics was the standard. In this *comedia* Cueva preferred Italianate verse forms, characterized by a line length of eleven syllables (*octava, estancia* and *terceto*) over Spanish forms of the eight-syllable lines. A marked use of those native Spanish meters, such as the eight-syllable, assonantal rhyme of the *romance,* had not come into vogue.

In *Comedia de la libertad de España por Bernardo del Carpio*, Cueva used only four verse forms. He favored the *octava* and the *redondilla,* adding *estancias,* and *tercetos* for lyrical variety. The *octava* is an Italianate strophe of eight-syllable lines rhyming AB AB AB CC. The *estancia* is a rhyming strophe of eleven- and seven-syllable lines of a variable length. Cueva's *estancias* are fourteen and thirteen lines long. The *terceto* is a stanza of three eleven-syllable lines, so interlocked that the second line rhymes with the first

---

[2] John W. Battle, "Dramatic Unity in the Plays of Juan de la Cueva," Diss. Duke 1970. Mr. Battle studied four plays and demonstrated that Cueva sought an intellectual reaction to moral issues through the use of rhetorical language, the varying of source materials, the parody of literary traditions, and the interweaving of reality and illusion.

and third lines of the following *terceto*, e.g. ABA BCB CDC. The *redondilla* is a Spanish stanza of four eight-syllable lines rhyming abba. A tabulation of the frequency of verse forms in this play is attached hereto as Appendix B.

One can make the following generalizations about Cueva's use of those forms in *Comedia de la libertad de España por Bernardo del Carpio*:[3]

1) Each act opens with an Italianate meter.
2) The play ends with *octavas*.
3) The *estancias* and *tercetos*, and occasionally the *octavas*, indicate lyrical monologues.
4) Narratives are cast in both *redondillas* and *octavas*.
5) The *octava* suggests solemnity, whereas the *redondilla* is used for a more rapid-paced dialogue and action.
6) Adaption of meter to speaker is not generally discernible, except that the four women characters are restricted to the use of the *redondilla*.

One can generalize on those meters individually:

1) The *octava* serves both as a narrative device and one for lyrical expression at a slow pace.
2) The *redondilla* serves to move the stage action at a more rapid pace.
3) The *estancia*, used twice, once by Tibalte and once by Carlo Mano, expresses a lofty, lyrical topic.
4) The *tercetos*, spoken by Alonso in monologue, reflect the serious thoughts of the speaker.

In addition, Cueva was effective in using figures of speech. The first two acts seem to be a preliminary warm-up exercise in rhetoric for the final two acts, for it is in the last acts in which the dramatist displays his discursive elegance. The basic schemes and tropes appear in the first two acts in a rudimentary form, becoming more polished in Acts III and IV.

A 'scheme' is a figure of speech which deviates from the normal word pattern. One can find in this play schemes of balance, of inverted word order, of omission, and of repetition. Representative of the scheme of

[3] Edwin S. Morby, "Notes on Juan de la Cueva: Versification and Dramatic Theory," *Hispanic Review*, 8 (1940), 213-18.

balance is Cueva's use of parallelism. The author uses it as a tool of advocacy.

In the following example, taken from Act II, Alonso has just accused Sancho of treason. The Count, awed by his king's glaring lack of mercy, attempts to persuade Alonso to reverse his decision to punish him. The last two lines of the quatrain are parallel in structure. The verb form precedes the subject in each clause, thereby stressing the action of the verb:

¿Es posible, gran señor,
que de tu gran magestad
se aparta la piedad
y te siga el cruel rigor?
(625-628)[4]

One further example comes from Act III. The king is alone on stage. In his monologue he states that he has pitted Bernardo against Carlo Mano and that he expects his nephew to be defeated by the powerful Emperor of the French. Each of the four lines begins with a verb, expressed as a command, followed by a clarifying phrase, which in three of the lines is the object of the action:

Salga, si ay brío en el que se lo vede;
defienda el reino que dessea por guerra;
eche de España la valía de Francia;
muestre en obras su orgullo y arrogancia.
(1223-1226)

Cueva achieves and maintains rhyme through inverted word order. This device occurs over ninety times, making it a hallmark of his style. It also presages a writing style which would become fashionable in the seventeenth century. This example is typical:

El fin de mi camino dirigido
acaba aquí; ya estoy puesto en Saldaña,

[4] Juan de la Cueva, *La libertad de España por Bernardo del Carpio*, ed. and intro. Anthony Watson, Exeter Hispanic Texts, No. 8 (Exeter, England: University Printing Unit, 1974). All further references to the text of the play come from this edition which is based on the first edition of the plays (1583).

del Cielo no a mi ruego consentido,
pues vendré a ver lo que mi alma daña.
(465-468)

Cueva changes the order of line 467 so that it rhymes with line 465 and so that all four lines contain eleven syllables. And in the following example, the order of line 1574 is changed, and all four lines contain eleven syllables:

Invencibles franceses, ya es llegado
el punto qu'el valor mostréis de Francia,
y aquel antiguo esfuerço que a domado
del mundo la sobervia y arrogancia.
(1571-1574)

As a scheme of omission, Cueva employs ellipsis for rhythm in the poetic line. In each of the following examples the poet omits the verb from the second line in order to preserve the eleven- and the eight-syllable lines respectively. The omitted forms appear in parentheses:

que aun la sombra del rey a de acatarse,
y el suelo qu'el rey pisa (a de) venerarse.
(335-336)

mas usas de tu poder,
en lugar d'armas, (usas) prisiones.
(1213-1214)

Cueva is versatile in the use of schemes of repetition. There are five different types of repetition within the text. In each of the cases this scheme emphasizes the dramatic situation. He uses anaphora, the repetition of the same word or group of words at the beginning of successive clauses, thirty times in the play. The following are representative:

Tuya es España, tuya es por derecho,
tuya se nombra, y dize sin jactancia
(1047-1048)

Triste de ti, Roldán. ¿Dó tu pujança?
¿Dó tu valor? ¿Dó está tu valentía?

¿Dó el encuentro temido de tu lança
(1699-1701)

Anadiplosis is the repetition of the last word of one clause at the beginning of the following one and occurs three times:

> Bien me lo sé el porqué, aunque no lo digo.
> No lo digo, ni es bien que yo lo diga,
> (8-9)

> qu'en un caso tan nuevo,
> nuevo efecto verás del que en mi vías!
> (349-350)

Cueva uses chiasmus, the reversal of grammatical structures in successive phrases or clauses, seven times. This scheme stands out more clearly to the eye than to the ear. In the phrases, "O entendimiento frágil, duro aprieto" (362), the two nouns are separated by their modifying adjectives. With "toquen caxas y pífaros resuenen" (1450), a verb in the command mode frames the beginning and the end of the line, while the noun subjects come side by side within the line. Another type of repetition is climax which occurs twenty times during the play. In these two examples the writer uses adjectives building in intensity as they near the noun:

> Duro, eterno, cruel, fiero cuidado (1)
> Larga, pesada, congoxosa vía (457)

Polyptoton is the repetition of words which are derived from the same root. This device seems to be Cueva's favorite form of repetition as he uses it more than forty times. For example:

> doña Ximena que tu ciego engaño
> engañó, que a llamar voy por su daño.
> (55-56)

Here the words *engaño*, a noun meaning "deceit," and *engañó*, the third person singular of the preterit tense meaning "it deceived," follow one another. The two words, derived from the same root, are spelled exactly the same, the accent alone distinguishing the noun from the verb. In the following example, Cueva shows how far he is willing to carry the device:

> que la fuerça del amor
> me fuerça con tanta fuerça,
> que él mesmo es el que esfuerça
>
> (429-431)

The root word is *fuerça* (power, force) in line 429. It is employed both as a verb (*fuerça*, it moves) and as a noun (*fuerça*, power) at line 430, and later a variation in the verb *esfuerça* (it compels, it moves). The repetition appears in a confession of love by doña Oliva to her beloved Tibalte and emphasizes that she is completely controlled by a force outside herself, by Love.

A 'trope' is a figure of speech in which a word is made to deviate from its ordinary meaning. Cueva employs five tropes consistently throughout the four acts. These are metaphors, similes, metonomy, rhetorical questions, and oxymoron. In addition, one example of onomatopoeia can be found in the play.

Cueva employs more than forty metaphors. Tibalte uses the first when he describes Ximena as "ardiéndose consigo en el infame/fuego" (51-52). The *infame fuego* is Love, which consumes the woman's life. Near the end of the play a direct comparison is drawn between Spain and a tomb, as Carlo Mano declares "¡O España, sepoltura/de la valía de Francia" (1777-1778), for indeed all of the prowess of France had been laid to rest in Spain.

Similes occur only twice, and both times they center around the image of Aeolus, King of the Winds. Ximena declares herself to be "qual roca . . . en medio/a la Eólica porfía" (115-116). The other simile describes Roldán's arrival at the court of Carlo Mano, "Con más presteza qu'el ligero viento/de la Eólica cárcel desatado" (1363-1364). In the first simile, Ximena imagines herself a rock buffeted by the fierceness of a strong wind. In the second, Roldán's movement is as rapid as that of the wind.

Metonomy, the substitution of a part for the whole, occurs nineteen times within the play. For example, Alonso refers to his kingdom with the phrase "mi onoroso ceptro" (271) where the scepter is an image meaning "kingdom." Suero refers to the force necessary to free Sancho as "el azero" (800).

Cueva uses the rhetorical question twenty-nine times. By means of this device the dramatist seeks indirectly to assert or to deny something. Count

Tibalte asks rhetorical questions in his speech on friendship in an attempt to emphasize constancy:

> ¿Soy menos yo? ¿Es menos conocida
> mi gloria? ¿Es menos firme mi desseo
> con el Conde, que Eurîalo con Niso?
> (382-384)

When the grandees approach Bernardo with the call to lead the Spaniards against the French, the questions suggest irrefutably that only he can save Spain:

> ¿A quién le toca sino a ti este hecho?
> ¿A quién sino tú podrá impedir a Francia
> la possessión? ¿Quién puede sin tu pecho
> domar su fiera y bárbara arrogancia?
> (1043-1046)

Thirty-two examples of the use of oxymoron, the linking of two contradictory words, are readily apparent in the play. Such phrases are *sabroso tormento* (58) and *dulce alivio* (95). These are used in the scene involving Ximena and Oliva and emphasize Ximena's confused state of mind brought on by the influence of Love.

The one example of onomatopoeia is the word *taratantara*. Roldán uses it to present a graphic picture of the battlefield where banners flutter and martial music echoes through the air:

> Sólo nos resta acometer de presto,
> que los contrarios vienen denodados,
> los estandartes tremolando al viento,
> dando ya el taratantara su aliento.
> (1607-1610)

Decorum, the insistence that the language and actions of a character reflect his social position, is a constant concern of Cueva in his *Exemplar poético*. A king is expected to speak in lofty language as befits his office; and when a messenger addresses the king, he must adapt his speech to the court (649-651). For the most part Cueva adheres to decorum in *Comedia de la libertad de España por Bernardo del Carpio*. For example, when a messenger arrives at Alonso's palace from France, he uses the more dignified *octava* to relate Carlo Mano's reaction to Alonso's revocation of the promise of accession.

> Cansaréte, señor, si represento
> con los propios efectos la sangrienta
> ira en que se encendió quando tu mando
> vio que Bernardo iva derogando.
>
> (1343-1346)

Cueva rises above slavish adherence to decorous rules, however, when to do so enhances the telling of the tale. For example, when the messengers arrive to herald the imminent approach of the French forces, Alonso, caught up in the emotion of the moment, eschews his elegant eleven-syllable lines to use the shorter eight-syllable line used by ordinary people:

> Correo Que salgas a socorrellos,
> porque su crueza estraña
> promete arruinar a España
> y que a empeçado por ellos.
> Rey Bolved, dezid que al momento
> mi socorro llegará,
> y al enemigo hará
> que mude el nefario intento.
>
> (1471-1478)

Cueva uses rhetorical devices to ornament his poetry, as well as for advocacy. Those devices are technical in nature, aimed at pleasing aurally.

The dramatist must also keep his audience entertained with a story. The playwright uses the technique of restatement to inform the audience of events which are taking place, or have taken place, away from the sight and sound of the stage. Storytellers as remote as Homer and as recent as writers of popular television series are deeply aware of the importance of restatement. Prefiguration is an author's way of informing the audience of an action or a character trait and its possible outcome. Activation occurs when the author carries out the plan earlier signaled or uses the trait previously established. Recapitulation is the retelling of an incident or the repeating of a theme or characteristic as a means of reminding the audience of those important elements. Cueva took advantage of this technique in *Comedia de la li-*

bertad de España por Bernardo del Carpio to keep certain themes, events, and character traits before his public.

The theme of injustice is one of the most important ideas that Cueva chose to emphasize and is used recurringly throughout the first three acts in a particularly artistic manner. Cueva employs this theme in much the same way as a musician would in composing a fugue. The subject is introduced, developed, recapitulated, and concluded. Injustice sounds for the first time near the end of Act I, when Ximena informs her brother that his behavior, particularly his refusal to hear her plea of innocence, is unjust. The theme reappears near the end of Act II when Sancho declares Alonso's pronouncement of treason to be unjust. When Sancho's eyes have been gouged out, he calls upon God to punish Alonso for his unjust deeds.

After he introduces the theme, Cueva turns to develop, recapitulate, and conclude it in Act III. Suero Velásquez and Velasco Meléndez sorrow for the plight of their relative, Sancho, who has received the brunt of Alonso's injustice. Their choice of vocabulary underscores the subject. References to the monarch are made in such terms as: *sin consejo; rigor áspero e inclemente; Rey severo; fiero, riguroso y cruel castigo*. These are strong words which paint a vivid picture of a merciless ruler.

Constantly repetitious references to the King's act of punishing Sancho emphasize the injustice. The phrases "más cruel que Nero [sic]" (1022), "una maldad la más terrible/que intentó hombre" (1025-1026), and the words *desconcierto* and *injusto* are heaped upon the previous ones, planting in one's ear and mind the extent to which the monarch has carried the punishment. *Desconcierto* implies a lack of interior harmony. *Injusto* is an outright declaration. Bernardo adds such descriptive words as *maldad, crueza* and phrases such as "fiereza en coraçón de fiera tan terrible" (1053-1054) and "¡O injusto Rey! ¡O manda injusta y vana/que al justo y puro ánimo inquieta" (1063-1064). Urraca recapitulates the theme when she tells the youth how his parents had been treated *contra ley*, and that through this act the king means to disinherit him. Bernardo, in four empathic lines, reminds the reader of the theme:

¡O Rey fiero, o Rey tirano,
Rey injusto, Rey cruel,
Rey sobervio, Rey infiel,
Rey sin ley, Rey mal christiano!
(1203-1206)

For further emphasis Cueva reemploys variations on the theme —*injusto intento* (1244), *injustamente* (1254), and "qu'es injusticia/hazer a Francia tan injusta manda" (1263-1264), "injusto y duro captiverio" (1274), "No es ley palabra injusta ser guardada" (1282). Constant reiteration, suggestion, and reentry of the theme impress it upon the audience. Through repetition of the injustices which Alonso has perpetrated, Cueva wants to emphasize that this is a vice which must be avoided.

As the art of theatrical writing developed, dramatists began to include instructions for the actors involved in the movement on stage. In the *princeps* Cueva supplies no explicit stage directions. Later editors of Cueva's plays have added the words *vase* or *vanse* for the appropriate exits. Cueva does, however, incorporate into the speeches of the actors on-stage action and suggestions of off-stage action.

Cueva's skillful indication of movement is exemplified by the following dialogue between Velasco and Suero. At lines 880-915 the grandees resolve to enlist the two nuns in their cause. Their words indicate both the stage scenery and their own actions:

Vel. Aquêste es el camino; ¡sus partamos!
(884)

. . .

Vel. Ten silencio, que aquêsta es la posada
de las beatas que buscando vamos.
Toca essa puerta; llama, llama rezio.
Suer. No oyen, aunque más el golpe arrezio.
Vel. Que no te ayan oído no me espanto,
porque estarán en su oratorio puestas
en disciplina o en ayuno santo
o en oración en solo Dios traspuestas.
Dêxame a mí llamar; desvíate un tanto.
Suer. No des tan grandes golpes, que molestas.
Vel. Pues, ¿cómo me an de oír, si no an oído?
Suer. Sí, an, que ya an de dentro respondido.
(887-898)

The movement is graphic as the two men move down the street and find the door of the convent. When Velasco succeeds in rousing the two women, the taciturn María inquires from behind the closed door "¿Quién llama aſ?" (899). When the gentlemen identify themselves, she becomes convinced that they are honorable. She asks them to wait a moment to be received and then greets them "Dios sea con vos, señores" (915).

In the *Exemplar poético* written some twenty-seven years after he produced his plays, Cueva applauds the fact that then contemporary Spanish dramatists felt free to disregard the classical unities of time and place (III, 499-501). He feels that was necessary to free drama from stilted plots. *Comedia de la libertad de España por Bernardo del Carpio* demonstrates the break with a tradition that demanded that those unities be followed. The unity of place required that a drama have only one setting. Cueva places the action in three distinct cities or areas of Spain: León, Saldaña, and Roncesvalles.

In similar manner Cueva dispenses with the unity of time which dictates that the action of a dramatic work transpire within twenty-four hours. In a few lines Cueva manages to leap over hours, days, months, and even years. For example, the interval between Acts III and IV is long enough for a messenger to take Bernardo's letter to and from Carlo Mano's court in France (ll. 1323-1330). In addition, during that time the hero has enlisted forces of Marsil, Moorish king of Zaragoza (1459-1462).

Cueva compresses the activities of weeks and months into 104 lines (1466-1570). In rapid succession messengers from Navarra and Biscaya report the advance of French forces, the sieges laid, and the cruelties imposed upon those areas. The French troops then appear at Roncesvalles and move into battle (1618). Only seventy-seven lines later, and it is the third and final day of the conflict.

Conclusion

As the dramatist molded this legend about Bernardo into a workable form, he was able to achieve flexibility and action which would have been impossible if he had allowed himself to be shackled by the traditional formalities. This was a declaration of independence for a playwright of the sixteenth century and a liberating influence for his successors.

Chapter IV
The Play — Its Characters

Cueva, never reluctant to experiment and invent, takes two liberties with characterization in order to facilitate audience understanding, to highlight character traits and action, and to impose his views upon the viewers. One device is to expand the importance or prominence of certain characters in the play over that which they occupied in the chronicles and legends. The other device is creation of characters who did not exist in the historical accounts but which he deems to be needed to achieve his goals of entertainment and advocacy.

Alonso

King Alonso is a strong, complex figure in this play. Leandro Fernández de Moratín appraised Alonso's character as "feroz, pusilánime, caviloso, inconsecuente y nulo."[1] Anthony Watson considers Alonso one of the best portrayed figures in Spain's early drama.[2] Cueva's Alonso indeed offers a fascinating study of a man who is in complete subjugation to his emotions. It

---

[1] Leandro Fernández de Moratín, *Orígenes del teatro español* (Buenos Aires: Editorial Schapire, 1946), p. 134. Hereafter Moratín.

[2] Juan de la Cueva, *La libertad de España por Bernardo del Carpio*, ed. and intro. Anthony Watson, Exeter Hispanic Texts, No. 8 (Exeter, England: University Printing Unit, 1974), p. vi: "The characters are clearly defined, especially that of Alfonso the Chaste, whose complex psychology makes him, in my view, one of the most interesting characters in pre-Lope de Vega drama." Hereafter Cueva.

is from Alonso, the central figure in the play, that the principal characters take their cues.

From the beginning of the drama, Cueva makes it exceedingly clear that Alonso's unbending code of honor motivates his deeds. Concern and worry envelop him day and night, granting him no respite:

> Duro, eterno, cruel, fiero cuidado,
> consumidor de todo mi reposo,
> por quien a tal estremo soy llegado
> que ni tengo descanso, ni reposo:
> ¿qué quieres más que verme en tal estado
> qual es en el que estoy, triste y penoso,
> sugeto a tu rigor y cruel castigo?
> (1-7)

Furthermore, these inner fears demand the punishment of offenders. A few lines later Alonso alludes to the treachery which he claims his sister, Ximena, and the Count of Saldaña, Sancho Días, perpetrated.

The audience does not become aware until the second scene that the secret marriage of Ximena and Sancho is the transgression that has precipitated the king's violent and unforgiving resentment. The secrecy of the ceremony which joined the couple, and their failure to obtain the king's permission and blessing, trigger his emotional response. Alonso deems the actions of Ximena and Sancho to be contemptuous and disrespectful to the Crown, as well as to his personal honor:

> ¿quién avrá que me culpe, si le duele
> mi mal? ¿Quién no dirá por que no vengo
> mi honor real, qu'es sólo el bien qu'estimo,
> pues d'él con tal afecto me lastimo?
> Más se dirá si dexo sin vengança
> tal maldad, tal insulto, tal engaño.
> (19-26)

Because Alonso fears that his reputation will suffer if he leaves the "insult" unavenged, he orders his sister brought to court. When she appears, already prejudged by her brother, Alonso refuses to listen to any excuse, saying "No ay disculpa en tal maldad" (196). He is resolute in that decision. Ximena reminds her brother that God avenges unjust deeds, but Alonso stubbornly believes that Heaven is on his side. He orders Ximena's removal to a convent. Alonso then turns his anger on Sancho Días. He calls on God to suspend divine mercy and, in a spirit of vengeance, to hurl thunderbolts from on high:

> ¡Ay, Dios, qu'estás desde tu trino assiento
> viendo el infando mundo que te ofende,
> sin que tu fuerte braço embíe el violento
> rayo qu'el suelo a castigar deciende,
> usa de tu poder; embía al momento
> el devido castigo que suspende
> tu divina piedad; toma vengança
> de tu ofensa en quien turba mi bonança!
>
> (273-280)

Alonso's unquenchable burning to punish his sister and her husband for their perceived disloyalty to the Crown has dominated his being. Deciding that death would in some way give Sancho repose, Alonso declares " . . .que en tristes agonías/vivas, y en congoxas fieras" (655-656). He then imposes a gruesome punishment and remains personally to oversee the blinding of Sancho.

Alonso's whole being is enveloped by a powerful and visceral hunger for retribution to the end that his emotions, uncontrolled and uncontrollable, have robbed him of mercy and reason. The blinding of Sancho is the nadir in a series of injustices perpetrated by a man who considers himself to be the ultimate just ruler and emphasizes the lack of discernment of this king who is himself blind to the truth.

The passage of time does little to increase Alonso's wisdom or to alleviate his strong feelings. Wearied by the burdens of ruling and by the politics of court, he thinks of stepping down. Having reared his nephew as his bastard son, he cannot bring himself to place Bernardo in line for the throne. He intrigues with Carlo Mano, emperor of the French, so as to deny Bernardo his rightful claim to succession.

Unfortunately, the king does not take into account that he is compromising the honor of Castile. Alonso's behavior is such that Sancho's kinsmen go so far as to liken his actions to that of the depraved Roman emperor Nero. When Bernardo confronts Alonso with his attempt to betray Spain and demands that his uncle mend his ways, he explains that the people prefer death to French rule. Bernardo does this, not for his own sake, but for the liberty and honor of the people of Castile. He urges his uncle to revoke his promise to Carlo Mano:

Esto, Rey no es traición, mas es justicia;
justicia pide, justa es su demanda;
justo es aquél que librar codicia
su cara patria de opresión infanda.
Mire su Magestad qu'es injusticia
hazer a Francia tan injusta manda;
derogue lo mandado tu potencia;
no veas tu reino en gálica obedencia.
(1259-1266)

Alonso responds that his word has been given and cannot be revoked, but Bernardo counters with "no es ley palabra injusta ser guardada" (1282). Alonso wants to stand by his promise made to Carlo Mano because he believes that he is doing the correct thing. But Alonso's idea of what is proper has made him unwittingly commit treason against his country. Bernardo convinces his uncle that his only alternative is to revoke the treacherous agreement with France. Alonso decides that his nephew's advice deserves consideration, and, surprisingly he relents. Alonso realizes that to continue on this course will result in disgrace for himself and perhaps loss of his country. Destructive as his conduct has been, the king cannot risk loss of his reputation nor of his homeland when once he understands the consequences of his treason. Other changes in the monarch's character follow. His decision to reverse himself is rapid and dramatic.[3]

At the beginning of Act IV, Bernardo pleads the cause of his parents, calling upon the ruler to imitate God by showing mercy. Alonso promises to yield to his nephew's urging. The compassionate change in Alonso in granting Bernardo's earnest and loving petitions can be viewed as miraculous repentance. This harsh man who has roared at God to render violent punishment upon Ximena and Sancho yields to the gentle suasion of his nephew who has invoked the image of a merciful God.

---

3 Alonso undergoes a rapid transformation similar to that of other characters in the early Spanish drama, namely the Marqués in Bartolomé de Torres Naharro's *Comedia Himenea* (1516) and Casandra in Gil Vicente's *Auto de la sibila Casandra* (1513).

Bernardo

Bernardo does not appear on stage until halfway through Act III. Prior to his entrance, however, he has been the subject of considerable discourse. Alonso, considering the young man an unworthy successor to the throne, purposes to give the throne to Carlo Mano. Suero Velásquez and Velasco Meléndez, who ardently oppose the king's plan, see that Bernardo learns of Alonso's machinations. Becoming enraged at Alonso's treason, Bernardo cannot accept the betrayal of Spain and agrees to lead the Spanish forces against the French.

From this point on, Bernardo assumes the cloak of a liberator. He swears to Heaven that he will defend Castile from French domination:

Y assí levanto al Cielo aquesta mano,
y al mesmo Dios le juro, afirmo y digo
de ser defensa al reino castellano
contra el furor del gálico enemigo.
Y digo más: de ser a Carlo Mano
cruel verdugo por el reino amigo,
y libertar mi patria, dando muestra
del valor que govierna aquesta diestra.

(1083-1090)

In these few lines Cueva prepares the audience to accept the pious young man as a potential leader in the liberation of Spain.

Bernardo, initially outraged when he finds out about Alonso's plan, manages to quell his rage, and then he is able to reason with his uncle effectively. Interestingly, Leandro Fernández de Moratín found in this confrontation reason to describe Bernardo in uncomplimentary terms. He wrote that Bernardo is "un baladrón temerario que insulta al rey su tío y amenaza a todo el universo."[4] In this writer's opinion, Bernardo del Carpio, in his confrontation with his uncle, showed himself to be an uncommonly stable and rational young man in the face of high provocation.

Bernardo reinforces his stance as champion of liberty throughout the final act. He tells various messengers to report to the Spanish forces that they need have no fear, for he will lead them to victory over the French. Gradual-

[4] Moratín, p. 134.

ly he assumes an heroic role as he promises that he will destroy the enemy. His intent is conveyed in such phrases as "Satisfaré con obras la insolencia/del francés" (1463-1464) and "Prometo domar, señor,/sus sobervias arrogancias" (1521-1522).

Bernardo strives to prevent the subjugation of his country, exercising nearly superhuman strength to expel personally the northern intruders. In this light, he is not the "braggart" whom Moratín belittled, but rather a patriot. A warrior-liberator, he fights the cream of Carlo Mano's army, and one by one he kills three superior officers, all members of the famous Twelve Peers. After he kills Roldán, he addresses the French corpses:

> Assí saldréis de la española guerra,
> insolentes franceses, destroçados
> de la invencible y victoriosa tierra
> do los famosos son despedaçados.
> La ira ardiente que mi pecho encierra
> me lleva con furor a que assolados
> sean por mí aquestos atrevidos,
> hasta qu'en polvo sean reduzidos.
>
> (1763-1770)

He thus demonstrates through words and deeds that he is fully conscious of his physical and inner strength and intends to use all his power to rid Spain of the enemy.

In the chronicles and ballads, Bernardo's personality is marked by his patriotism and by his love for his father. Cueva stresses the role of Bernardo as the patriot, with diminution of the importance of the father-son relationship. Bernardo sets his priorities according to the most urgent need, placing his country above family and self. The future of Spain is in the balance and is far more pressing than the future of his parents. Bernardo aids Alonso in doing his duty as ruler, because he knows that for both himself and the king, affairs of state must take precedence over personal matters.

At the conclusion of the drama Bernardo moves from the level of a mere mortal to that of an immortal hero when he is crowned by Marte. In the apotheosis of the hero as a second Marte, Cueva clearly gives him heroic qualities: bravery, trustworthiness, steadfastness, and a firm belief in liberty.

Carlo Mano

Cueva does not significantly alter the chronicle image of Carlo Mano. The dramatist portrays him as King of France and disregards the fact that he was also the Holy Roman Emperor. Cueva's description of Carlo Mano's behavior closely parallels the description of the deportment of his Spanish counterpart. Both loved self and power to the detriment of their subjects. Long before Carlo Mano's first appearance on the stage, the audience envisions an angry, proud, and powerful man, determined to destroy those who dare to oppose his will. The viewer is not surprised then when soon after Act IV begins, a messenger from the French court describes Carlo Mano's furious response to Alonso's retraction of his concession to the French king.

Carlo Mano has sent a reply filled with anger and hatred. He insists that Alonso must consent to become a vassal of France. Should the Spaniards continue with their insolence, then they must face the prospect of a fierce war:

> Apercíbete a la guerra,
> porque te quiero avisar
> que hombre no pienso dexar
> que quede vivo en tu tierra.
>
> (1431-1434)

Carlo Mano's overbearing arrogance is further emphasized by the report by a Spaniard that the French ruler swears utterly to destroy the people of Spain.

Subsequently Carlo Mano speaks to his troops immediately before the battle of Roncesvalles to kindle within them the fire of patriotism and to arouse their *esprit de corps*. He declares that the Pyrenees are behind them and that they now have no alternative but to pursue the conquest of Spain. The emperor's willingness to sacrifice his troops for his own ends is demonstrated as he threatens the army with the Pyrenees as an impassable obstacle at their backs.

The ensuing battle is a great disaster for the French. A captain in that army decries the ruler's greed which has caused the tremendous loss:

> ¡Ay codicia, que a tanto mal inclina!
> ¡Ay Carlos, de tu reino pestilencia,

quánto mejor en tu quietud vivieras
sin qu'el reino de España pretendieras!
(1663-1666)

The selection of the name Carlo Mano for the historical Carlo Magno (Charles the Great or Charlemagne) provided Cueva with an interesting double entendre. In addition to creating a transparent pseudonym for the real French emperor, the writer uses the word "mano" to suggest the hand of Charlemagne poised and ready to seize Iberia. Whether Cueva created the pun with tongue in cheek or whether he used the allusion to engender patriotic feelings is not clear. Considering the extreme patriotism of Cueva — described by Glenn as one of Seville's greatest chauvinists[5] — one is inclined to the view that the author used the word "mano" purposefully and seriously. This analysis is reinforced by the haunting words spoken by the Emperor who was grievously moved by the carnage which his ambition had wrought:

¡Ay, Carlos, Carlos, ya no Carlo Mano,
ya no el qu'el mundo le tenía respeto,
ya no el que fue de todos tan temido,
(1786-1788)

He thus is no longer Charles the Great, nor the Charles whose hand hovered menacingly over Spain, but rather, simply Charles. With these poignant words, the saddened and repentant emperor returns to France.

Ximena

Ximena exists only as a name in the traditional accounts concerning Bernardo del Carpio. Cueva breathes life into this woman, portraying her in terms of courtly love. Before Cueva brings Ximena to the stage, he gives the audience a foreshadowing of her character. Count Tibalte, in a monologue, muses that she is a slave of her emotions. Indeed she burns with a passion which she calls *sabroso tormento* (58). It consumes her to the point that she gets no rest, even as her brother Alonso gets no rest because of his being con-

[5] Richard F. Glenn, *Juan de la Cueva* (New York: Twayne Publishers, 1973), p. 17: "Seville never produced a greater chauvinist than Juan de la Cueva."

sumed with a passion to vindicate the injury to his reputation as he perceived it. The audience observes her, as pining for her absent husband, she tries to verbalize her innermost sentiments:

> No hallo medio en mi mal,
> que qualquiera me condena,
> me oprime, fuerça y refrena,
> me lastima y tiene tal.
> Si en tal estado me veo,
> combatida triste assí,
> conjurados contra mí
> ausencia, amor y desseo,
> ¿qué valor ay, qué prudencia
> tan bastante que resista
> el rigor de tal conquista,
> si está la gloria en ausencia?
> Nada puede aprovecharme,
> todo me causa temor,
> y aquello que no es amor,
> es dolor para acabarme.
>
> (73-88)

Doña Oliva, Ximena's confidante, echoes the combat imagery by calling Ximena's agitated emotional state "una lid" (103). The princess regrets that no remedy exists for the storm that rages within. Cueva uses a graphic simile to demonstrate the extent to which love exerts its influence in Ximena's life "que qual roca estoy en medio/a la Eólica porfía" (114-115). While Ximena remains constant and steadfast in her love for Sancho she undergoes incessant pressures, as though she is continually buffeted by the strongest of winds, here symbolized by Aeolus, King of the Winds.

In the descriptive scene (ll. 57-128) which introduces Ximena to the audience, Cueva shows the vexations caused by her lover's prolonged absence. Although her beloved lives away from her, Ximena nurtures her love for Sancho with the hope that he will someday return to her.

Ximena appears to live in her own world without any appreciation of the damage she has done herself with Alonso, even though her confidante Doña Oliva has attempted on one occasion to alert her to the danger. When summoned to appear before the king, she is composed. As he rails at her, she, apparently for the first time, realizes that she will be held accountable for her clandestine marriage. Even then this gentle woman naively believes that her own brother will forgive her or at least deal leniently with her romantic indiscretion:

> ningún yerro se comete
> que no pueda disculparse
> (197-198)

Ximena and her brother Alonso were cut from the same bolt, each propelled by almost irrational emotion. Oblivious to the consequences, she exalted her own happiness by marrying in secret without royal sanction. Her brother's egomania requires him to punish her and Sancho with a harsh severity not merited by the offense; and even as she is banished, her warm mother's love compels her to entreat the king on her son's behalf. Ximena, it may be said, loved well if not wisely.

Sancho

Cueva created a new role for Sancho Días. In the chronicles and in the ballads it is Sancho who shows concern for his son Bernardo and who calls upon Alonso for mercy to spare the child's life and to rear him at court. Sancho, as Cueva portrays him, does not reflect the suffering-father image found throughout the sources. Therein the writers underscore a profound love of father for son. Cueva reverses the portrayals of Sancho and Ximena from those in the histories and in the ballads. Ximena becomes the parent concerned about the son's welfare. She pleads with Alonso that he send for Bernardo so that the boy may enjoy the opportunities provided at the court. In the play Sancho never refers to his son.

The audience meets Sancho late in the second act, after he has been the subject of much discourse. He warmly welcomes his friend Tibalte to Saldaña. Sancho asks Tibalte the purpose of his visit. When he hears that Tibalte carries a summons for him to appear at court, Sancho's keen sense of duty requires that he go to León even though death may await him there:

> ¿Dudó que yo su mando no cumpliesse,
> qual devo en fe de noble cavallero?
> Hágase lo que manda, que aunque viesse

a los ojos el fin horrible y fiero,
de mí será mi Rey obedecido,
siendo el mandado vuestro y d'él cumplido.
(531-536)

Cueva thus injects bitter irony in this speech, for Sancho's eyes will not be able to see the end, as they will be plucked out near the end of Act II.

Sancho is unaware of Alonso's anger. When the king explodes into a rage, demanding the count's head for his *crimen infando,* Sancho declares his innocence and subsequently pleads for mercy. Failing to persuade the king, he invokes divine retribution upon his tormentor. While one cannot resist feeling sorry for Sancho, neither can one overlook the defects of character which left him living apart from wife and son, neither of whom he so much as mentioned during his trial and agonizing punishment.

Tibalte

In the *PCG* and in the *CGE* the historians depict Tibalte only as one of the nobles who journeys to Saldaña to summon Sancho to return to the court. In the play Cueva gives Tibalte a more distinct personality and a more distinctive function. He acts as Alonso's intermediary both to Ximena and to Sancho. This royal messenger carries out his orders to escort first the princess and later the count to the royal palace. His loyalties are severely tested when he must escort his close friend, Sancho, to the court at León, as he is aware of the consequences which await Sancho there. The conflicting pull of loyalty to the king and loyalty to friend wrenches Tibalte. At last, Tibalte decides that his friend Sancho must be saved from the king's wrath. When the time comes for him to stand by Sancho, Tibalte shows that his expressions of friendship were nothing more than empty rhetoric. He fails miserably as a friend in order to remain in Alonso's good graces.

This self-serving trait carries over into his relationship with the other characters with whom he comes in contact, namely Ximena and Tibalte's own lady-love, Doña Oliva. The courtier knows full well that the reason that Alonso summons Ximena to the royal presence is to mete out punishment to her but he feigns ignorance of Alonso's motive. Subsequently when he is sent to Saldaña to bring in Sancho, Tibalte falsely tells Oliva that the king has not informed him of the purpose of his mission.

Tibalte is a selfish courtier who prefers to follow the fortune of the most influential person he knows, rather than to disrupt the *status quo* and bring uncertainty upon his future. The dramatic character of Tibalte is summed up in lines which he speaks near the end of Act II:

> Qual, señor, de ti es mandado
> de mí será obedecido,
> y sin discrepar cumplido
> todo tu real mandado.
> (697-700)

Tibalte, perhaps more than any other character, reflects the human condition. One can empathize with him when he struggles to decide whether to warn Sancho to flee; and one can sorrow with him when he elects the easy way.

Doña Oliva

Cueva adds the relatively important character of Doña Oliva. She is pure invention on Cueva's part. She serves as confidante to Ximena and lady-love to Tibalte. These postures provide an interesting balance. As confidante she is the alter ego of Ximena, living with her and supporting her when she feels buffeted by the winds which separate her from Sancho. In her role as Tibalte's mistress, Oliva represents the opposite of Ximena. She and Tibalte, who are lovers, are free from the monarch's intervention, whereas Ximena and Sancho, while married, but having incurred the king's wrath, must live their lives apart.

Suero Velásquez
Velasco Meléndez

The roles of Suero Velásquez and Velasco Meléndez in the play differ only slightly from those in the sources. In the play, it is they who have learned of Alonso's pact with the French, and it is they who take the initiative to inform Bernardo of the deceit and to urge him to act promptly to dissuade the king from consummating the treaty.

Urraca Sánchez
María Meléndez

In the sources Suero and Velasco appeal to Urraca Sánchez and María Meléndez to reveal to Bernardo the true story of his birth and who his parents are. Without changing that action by Suero and Velasco, Cueva describes the women as nuns. This of itself gives the women and the task they perform greater significance, for in sixteenth-century Spain the Church and those bound to it in service exerted strong influence.

Roldán

The sources concur that Roldán, Carlo Mano's nephew and a member of the elite Twelve Peers, was killed in the battle at Roncesvalles. Cueva shows that he was acquainted with the legendary Roldán who, known as Orlando, was driven mad by his love for the beautiful Angelica.[6] In the play, Cueva presents Roldán as a powerful, valiant warrior, a loyal subject of his king, brave in the face of danger, and feared by his adversaries.

During the battle at Roncesvalles, Roldán, as an experienced commander, recognizes that France is being defeated, and he attributes the loss to Heaven's punishment. He refuses to allow the adverse tides of battle to deter him from seeking out Bernardo for personal combat. When the two meet, they hurl challenges at one another and then begin to duel. Moments later Roldán disarms Bernardo, and so as not to take unfair advantage, Roldán throws down his weapon. The ferocity of the fight does not slacken, and Bernardo strangles the Frenchman.

---

[6] Cueva, p. 56, note 31: "'aquél que la gloriosa/fama celebra' is, of course, Orlando/Roland and 'la bella dama' is Angelica." Also see Thomas Bullfinch, *Legends of Charlemagne* (London: J. M. Dent; New York: E. P. Dutton, 1924), pp. 22-30, 108-123 for details of how Angelica, daughter of the king of Cathay, captured the hearts of all the Peers, and how her marriage to Medoro caused Roland (Orlando) to lose his reason.

While Carlo Mano represents the worst of the French, Roldán represents the best. In the face of adversity, he asks Heaven's pity but even then puts himself in harm's way. Only a hero would cast away his sword. Roldán is a hero of major proportions cast in a minor role.

Marte

The final important character is Marte, Roman god of War, whom Cueva borrowed from Roman mythology. Marte terminates the *comedia* with an epilogue in which he rewards Bernardo for his heroic efforts. When he places a crown of laurel on Bernardo's brow, he symbolically bestows divine blessings upon the hero.

Conclusion

Juan de la Cueva saw the legend of Bernardo del Carpio as a story line for creating a play for the time and place in which he lived. Without being bound by details of history nor by rules of formal composition, he expanded and fashioned a drama, part fiction and part history. He created entirely new characters, and he liberally changed both actions by and personalities of historical figures. Using these real and imaginary characters, he wove into the fabric of the drama certain of his own patriotic, moral, and religious principles.

Chapter V
The Play as Literature and as Entertainment

Cueva, in *Comedia de la libertad de España por Bernardo del Carpio*, is innovative in his writing techniques; that is, he is creative in the way in which he arranges the words and develops the plot, and in his portrayal of characters. These techniques alone would have lifted this *comedia* above plays of that period written for simple diversion, but taking it further out of the ordinary (of that time) was the writer's use of this dramatic offering as a vehicle to influence readers and viewers.

Some Hispanists are reluctant to concede Cueva's influence upon subsequent Spanish dramatists, regarding it as folly to suggest that Cueva could have affected writers such as Lope de Vega.[1] Other Hispanists point out that Cueva's failure to speak of Lope, and Lope's failure to mention Cueva was intentional.[2]

---

[1] Rinaldo Froldi, *Lope de Vega y la formación de la comedia* (Salamanca: Anaya, 1973), p. 109: "Demasiado poco nos parece para considerar a Juan de la Cueva como el dramaturgo español de la segunda mitad del XVI y como el precursor de Lope de Vega."

Richard Glenn, *Juan de la Cueva* (New York: Twayne Publishers, 1973), p. 43: "To return to the fundamental question of his influence on Lope de Vega's dramatic art — an often-made claim must be refuted. The assertion that Cueva's introduction of Spanish history and national heroes on the stage paved the way for Lope's dramatization of the same material is specious."

[2] Juan de la Cueva, *El Infamador*, ed. Francisco A. de Icaza, Clásicos castellanos, 60 (Madrid: Espasa-Calpe, 1973), p. L: "Una de las mayores glorias de Juan de la Cueva es haber sido el iniciador y, en cierto modo, el maestro de Lope. Y

Cueva created or pioneered several new techniques which Lope apparently adopted, refined, and improved. One cannot disregard the fact that Cueva started new trends by finding topical inspiration in Spanish history, by disregarding the unities of time and place, and by composing dramas in polymetrical verse. In time, the disregard of the unities of time and place and the composition of plays in polymeter became the norm for Lope and the dramatists who followed. These were to last in the Spanish theater for at least a century. In addition, writers after Cueva often turned to an historical era to select a setting, characters, or an event for dramatization. This trend has lasted until our own day. The evidence seems to preponderate that Lope saw or read Cueva's plays and that he liked what he saw. It is clear that he used some of the same techniques, and it is more than less likely that he chose to emulate Cueva's style.

From all accounts it would appear that Lope spent some time in Seville around 1582, before going to Lisbon where, in 1583, he joined the armed force of the Marquis of Santa Cruz which sailed to the Azores to put down a rebellion.[3] He also visited in Seville at different times during 1600-1604.[4] Given the population of Spain at the time (7,000,000 to 8,000,000 inhabitants),[5] the population of Seville (150,000),[6] and the relatively small number of writers, it does not appear fanciful to suggest that Lope heard of Cueva, met him, or read or saw his plays.

Juan de la Cueva envisioned drama as a didactic tool through which he

---

ambos fingieron ignorarse, y en sus escritos no se nombraron jamás."

Hugo A. Rennert, *The Life of Lope de Vega (1562-1635)* (1904; rpt. New York: G. E. Stechert & Co., 1937), p. 336: ". . . the omission was doubtless intentional." Hereafter Rennert.

Humberto López Morales, *Tradición y creación en los orígenes del teatro castellano* (Madrid: Ediciones Alcalá, 1968), p. 24n11: "El silencio no fue un arma rara en manos de Lope de Vega; es con la que combate también a Juan de la Cueva."

3 Francis C. Hayes, *Lope de Vega* (New York: Twayne Publishers, 1967), p. 64: "Seville, Cadiz, and Lisbon were next on his itinerary in 1582, and the Azores in 1583, with the armed forces of the Marquis of Santa Cruz, to put down a rebellion."

4 Rennert, p. 148: ". . . he resided there (in Seville) for long periods from the close of 1600 to May, 1604, . . ."

5 Fernardo Lázaro Carreter, *Lope de Vega. Introducción a su vida y obra* (Salamanca: Anaya, 1966), p. 13: "En la época de Lope de Vega, España cuenta con ocho o nueve millones de habitantes, si incluimos 1.250.000 que corresponden al reino anexionado de Portugal."

6 Antonio Domínguez Ortiz, *Orto y ocaso de Sevilla*, 3a. edición, Colección de bolsillo, Número 31 (Sevilla: Publicaciones de la Universidad de Sevilla, 1981), p. 72: ". . . el total (de la población de Sevilla en 1588) debia aproximarse a las 150.000 almas."

could make political, moral, and religious statements while, at the same time, entertaining the public. Whereas Cueva was a creative playwright who greatly influenced subsequent writers, he did not seem to make a lasting impression on the general public.

Drama is presumably written to be performed. As an art form it comes to life when the costumed actors step before the audience to speak the lines and to portray characters by movement and expression. Lighting and set design help to create the illusion. The general audience attends such a spectacle with the expectation, or at least the hope, of being entertained. People wish to be transported to a make-believe environment in which others have problems or in which fantasies or romance or personal heroism may be indulged. The audience of sixteenth-century Spain doubtless shared such hopes and expectations with the audiences of ancient Greece and those of today. While critics may judge the literary or dramatic qualities of a play, ultimately success or failure is measured at the box office, and this in turn hinges upon how well the dramatist entertains. If the playwright wishes to teach, he must do so subtly, without losing sight of what Cueva, in *Exemplar poético*, described as the "delighting factor."

Juan de la Cueva was, then, well aware of the necessity to entertain. The correlative of the necessity to delight was, according to Cueva, that if the writer neither teaches (*enseñar*) nor pleases (*deleitar*), it is only fitting that his work be ignored (I, 304-309). One can only wonder whether Cueva perceived a flaw in his own work. He was not what modern critics would call a box-office success. His plays were produced, as far as is known, only in Seville during the late sixteenth century. From all accounts it appears that the plays were neither reworked nor produced again.

Subject matter was not the cause of his failure to attract an audience. The medieval legend of Bernardo del Carpio contains in abundance elements which could entertain, excite, or move an audience. Everyone loves a story of a popular, heroic figure who frees his country from the threat of foreign domination, particularly when he has had to overcome great obstacles to do so. Sixteenth-century Spaniards could be proud of their ancestor who had repelled the army of Europe's most powerful ruler centuries earlier. Spain had slowly gained political prominence in Europe and in those days had yet to be humiliated in defeat. Cueva chose well when he selected the story of Bernardo del Carpio for dramatization. In addition, thwarted love which overcomes evil has always been a favorite device of the creators of drama or fiction. Plays which contains such components, while they may not always produce great theater, do often account for box-office success.

Cueva, given such ingredients in the legend of Bernardo, was either unwilling or unable to translate them into a play which audiences demanded to see again.

The play could not have failed because it was too long. Its 1873 lines make it shorter than most of Cueva's fourteen plays. Another important factor contributing to the brief exposure of the play could have been that Cueva did not flesh out his skeletal drama, and the performance was over before the audience had become comfortable. *Comedia de la libertad de España por Bernardo del Carpio* contains no subplots which create interest or divert the audience's thoughts from the main action. Except for the early scene in which Ximena expounds on the turmoil in her life caused by Sancho's absence, romantic love as a theme has a secondary place. Cueva keeps the audience at a distance, so that its members act as judges listening to a debate rather than as participants in an adventure.

Style exerts a major influence on the reader or viewer. Cueva's language was geared to an intellectual, and even elitist, audience, not to the common Spaniard. Although the speeches are not necessarily dull, and at times even become lyrical, Cueva's writing, one must admit, seems heavy-handed, and the play itself at times ponderous. More than half of the lines in this play are eleven syllables long. These lines cause the speeches to take on a serious mien and move at a slower pace than would the use of eight-syllable lines. This movement is much like background music in a motion picture. The slower lines can be compared to an adagio or largo movement which lends dignity and solemnity to the action. Too much solemnity can lose an audience, especially in a play concerning military victory in successful defense of the nation and of freedom. Greater use of eight-syllable lines might have provided a brisker tempo, although even that meter falls short of movement commensurate with martial music. If one may borrow once more from the musical arts for comparison, the rhetorical devices used in a play may be compared to the orchestration of background music. The heavy brass and lower strings must be balanced with instruments which give brilliance and color. The style of a writer affects not just what the listener hears but also how he hears it. Style can clarify the writer's message, or it can obscure it. In this play, if Cueva was writing for mass entertainment, his writing style defeated his aim. If his targeted audience was the literati, he was successful. Nothing shows that success so much as the emulation of his literary devices by authors who came later.

Chapter VI
The Play — Its Public and Personal Themes

Juan de la Cueva's fourth play, *Comedia de la libertad de España por Bernardo del Carpio*, holds a special fascination for serious inquiries into early Spanish literature, and particularly for those drawn to the Spanish theater and its development. This play, which dramatizes the story of Bernardo and his struggle to drive the French from Spain, does more than simply perpetuate those events. It has in recent years received closer attention than it might warrant as a drama or solely as history. Literary historians have often mentioned it as one of Cueva's three dramas based upon Spanish history, but there, for the most part, commentary stopped. The first serious attention given it, was in 1971, when Anthony Watson interpreted it as a political allegory of the 1570s.

In *Comedia de la libertad de España por Bernardo del Carpio*, Cueva conveys several messages at different levels. The author was a solemn man, not much given to whimsy, and his serious nature is reflected throughout this play. Cueva was intensely loyal to his country, to his sense of morality, and to the church. Each of these propensities is discernible, and each forms a part of the thematic structure of the play.

The Public Themes — Patriotic and Political

Patriotism is an important theme in *Comedia de la libertad de España por Bernardo del Carpio*. Bernardo represents the true patriot who puts aside his personal interest in order to save his country. When he is told that his uncle has committed a treasonous act by inviting Carlo Mano to become his successor, Bernardo quickly steps forward to offer his services in defense of the country. And when he learns that the king has treated his parents wrongly, Bernardo continues to place the concerns of Spain above his own problems. He cannot and will not allow his country to be betrayed, even though the king has dealt a series of harsh blows to him personally. Bernardo expresses the indomitable Spanish spirit when he tells a messenger from Navarre that the French will soon realize that invasion will not come easily for them. The young hero makes good on his promise when he decimates the enemy force. When at last he has sent the French fleeing, Bernardo urges his countrymen to sing the glories of their nation:

¡Ea, varones del esperio suelo,
a quien el Cielo ofrece immortal gloria,
ceñid de lauro las sagradas frentes
y canten vuestra gloria todas gentes!
(1862-1865)

Cueva's brand of patriotism is at once simple and sophisticated. He has a deep and genuine love for his country, and he does not seem overly influenced by pageantry and the trappings of power. Cueva's love of Spain and his concern that his ruler, Philip II, control his urge to invade Portugal is the subject of a monograph by Anthony Watson.[1] In that study Watson interprets nine of Cueva's dramas as the playwright's means of advising his king to stay out of Portuguese politics and to let the Portuguese decide for themselves who should be their king. One of those nine plays is *Comedia de la libertad de España por Bernardo del Carpio,* and Watson suggests that this particular play was the most persuasive of all of Cueva's plays, as Ocampo's chronicle of the story of Bernardo bore uncanny resemblance to the later

[1] Anthony Watson, *Juan de la Cueva and the Portuguese Succession* (London: Tamesis Books, 1971). Hereafter Watson.

political events in the Iberian Peninsula. In Cueva's time, there was a strong belief that history tended to repeat itself.[2]

The tensions over the question of the Portuguese succession began in early August of 1578. In July of that year, King Sebastian of Portugal invaded Morocco with high hopes of destroying the Islamic infidel. At Alcazar-Kebir on August 4, 1578, the Moroccans soundly defeated the Portuguese. Sebastian was among the dead. The young king — he was only twenty-five — had not married, nor had he named a successor. The throne passed to Sebastian's great-uncle, Cardinal Henry, old, unmarried, and sick. The question of succession became of greater importance. Henry had three choices: (1) the Duchess of Braganza, his niece, (2) Philip II, his nephew, and (3) Antonio, Prior of Crato, his illegitimate nephew. For a time Henry favored his niece as the successor but changed his mind in favor of Philip.

Antonio was the natural son of Prince Luiz, Cardinal Henry's brother, and a low-born Jewess, Violante Gomes. Antonio claimed that his parents had been married in secret and that he was the rightful heir. Antonio, who favored protecting Portugal from Spanish aggression, was popular with the common people in Portugal and with many Spaniards, especially those living in Seville. Cardinal Henry appeared to hate Antonio, whose licentious behavior offended his chaste uncle.

Philip II, who was Sebastian's uncle, hoped that in acceding to the Portuguese crown, he could fulfill the dream of Ferdinand and Isabella which was to consolidate the Iberian Peninsula under a single monarch. Of the three contenders for the approval of Henry, Philip was the most powerful and the apparent choice of the Cardinal-King. Before he made his decision, however, Henry died in January, 1580. Philip was ready to invade Portugal. On August 15, 1580, Philip's army, under the command of the Duke of Alba, defeated a small, poorly-equipped Portuguese army near the Portuguese town of Alcantara. Philip entered Lisbon in early December, and in April, 1581, he was sworn in as King Philip I of Portugal by the parliament assembled at Thomar. Portugal remained as part of Spain until 1640 when the seventh Duke of Braganza led a non-violent coup which restored Portuguese independence.[3]

---

[2] Watson, p. 4: "In sixteenth-century Europe the belief was almost universally held that history repeats itself and that the events of the past could consequently be used to determine what kind of political behavior was advisable in the present."

[3] The following histories have been helpful in understanding the Portuguese annexation:

A. H. de Oliveira Marques, *History of Portugal* (New York and London: Colum-

In his reading of the play as political allegory, Watson perceives that Alonso is a disguise for Cardinal Henry; Bernardo for Antonio, Prior of Crato; and Carlo Mano for Philip II. Watson is convinced that members of the audience, aware of the king's desire to wear the Portuguese crown, would have drawn close parallels between Cardinal Henry and Alonso. Alonso, as well as Henry, was chaste and obsessed with preserving family honor.[4] The comparison of Bernardo to Antonio was not so close. The parallel between Carlo Mano and Philip was that each, in his respective era, was the most powerful monarch in Europe. Bernardo's victory over the powerful French seems to be a message to Philip that might does not make right, and that if Spain

> enters into a private agreement with another monarch against the will of his people; a popular patriot may emerge to lead the Portuguese people to another Aljubarrota as Bernardo led his people to Roncesvaux.[5]

Watson's interpretation of this play reveals scholarly research into the complexities of politics and its possible influence on Cueva so as to move the playwright to adapt Bernardo's history for the stage. Watson calls this "Cueva's best play,"[6] and this writer agrees. This writer also is willing to accept Watson's thesis that Cueva wrote with the aim in mind of dissuading Philip from invading Portugal, but is not willing to assume that political intercession was Cueva's sole object of persuasion.

The Personal Themes — Moral and Religious

Cueva was orthodox in his morality and in his religion. An examination of *Comedia de la libertad de España por Bernardo del Carpio* reveals strong

---

bia University Press, 1972), I, 306-15, 322-9.

R. Trevor Davies, *The Golden Century of Spain 1501-1621* (London: Macmillan and Co., 1937), pp. 184-93.

4 Watson, p. 82: "In addition to this (that the Prior of Crato was the fruit of a union between Prince Luiz and Violante Gomes), Antonio was notorious for the licentious life he was accustomed to lead and the Cardinal, who had observed the strictest chastity throughout his life, found this particularly unforgivable."

5 Watson, p. 93.

6 Watson, p. 98.

moral and religious undergirding. Cueva's first signal of his intention in this regard is found in the preface to his plays, the "Epístola dedicatoria a Momo." In that prose epistle he exhorts his readers to recognize the importance of the virtues of temperance, fortitude, justice and prudence ("Templança, Fortaleza, Justicia i Prudencia"). He considers temperance — moderation in all things — to be the principal one. Cueva laments the fact that his virtue, once highly prized by the ancients, no longer holds its position of honor.

Relying upon ridicule — exemplified by his dedication of his plays to Momus, the pagan god of ridicule — he hopes to goad his contemporaries into embracing the excellence of virtuous living. In this manner, through diverse illustrations, the dramatist arrives at the didactic intent. He writes:

> . . . I à llegado la malicia de nuestros tiempos en algunos, a querer formar escrupulo de afrenta en la composicion dellas, sin considerar el prouecho que en la republica resulta de su letura. Pues la Comedia esimitacion de la Vida humana, espejo de las costumbres, retrato dela verdad, en que se nos representan las cosas que devemos huir, o las que nos conviene elegir, con claros i evidentes exemplos poderoso qualquiera dellos à confundir las cauilosas intenciones delos que condenan este genero de Poesia, . . .
>
> (1583 edition, folio 4 (unnumbered), recto)

A complete text of the dedicatory epistle is attached as Appendix C.

The metaphors which Cueva uses in the foregoing quotation — an imitation, a mirror, a portrait — point out that he wants to disclose to his audience a truth or truths often overlooked in the process of day-to-day living. To accomplish that, the illusion created on the stage must be so clear that the viewer will easily recognize the vices and virtues; and the dramatization must be so forceful as to persuade the viewer to avoid the vices and to embrace the virtues.

Juan de la Cueva follows that rule when he writes *Comedia de la libertad de España por Bernardo del Carpio*. Therein he dramatizes the near devastating effects of the vices of intemperance and injustice.

Intemperance is the inability to control one's emotions. This vice exerts a major influence upon King Alonso. He permits the problems of everyday life to cloud his judgment as a king. When his delicate sense of family honor is threatened, his reaction is violent. He does not use reason to keep his passionate behavior in check. He allows the problems of Citizen Alonso to become those of King Alonso.

Alonso cannot distinguish the "body natural" from the "body mystical."[7] A ruler must project an image of equanimity and, therefore, his personal life cannot, and must not, infringe upon and affect the execution of his official duties. Alonso does just the opposite. He equates the secret marriage of his sister and Sancho Días with the crime of high treason.

Alonso's view of his role as king is distorted. The sixteenth-century preacher, Juan de Avila, warned against such behavior. When a ruler, Avila writes, turns his private affairs into the concerns of the state, he is forgetting his crucial role in society:

> . . . el buen público no se tenga cuenta con hacienda, salud, honra ni vida, cuando fuere menester offrecerlo todo por la buena execución de su officio. . . . Coraçón real y divino ha de tener, porque si lo tiene particular y encorvado hacia si mismo, no tiene parte en este negocio, pues con particular coraçón no se puede exercitar officio de persona pública. Professión es de hazer bien a muchos, aun con perdida propia; . . .[8]

---

[7] See Ernst Kantorowicz, *The King's Two Bodies: A Study in Medieval Political Theory* (Princeton: Princeton University Press, 1957.) Also William McCrary discusses this concept in his article, "Ritual Action and Form in *La Estrella de Sevilla*," in *Homenaje a William L. Fichter: Estudios sobre el teatro antiguo hispánico y otros ensayos* (Madrid: Editorial Castalia, 1971), p. 506: "To appreciate the centrality of the King is first to understand the *gemina natura* which so preoccupied the medieval jurists and moralists and their Renaissance continuators. As head of state, the prince, it was held, had two bodies: the body natural or personal, and the body corporate or mystical, i.e., the office. The distinction was necessary to differentiate between the privileges and limitations of a specific individual and those of the same individual invested with the responsibilities of the crown. Essentially it was an acknowledgement of the difference between genus and species. While the man wearing the crown would die, the office continued eternally resident in the body of the successor. The King, then, became the focal point on which the collective social consciousness reconciled the categorical mandate of continuity in the affairs of men with the empirical observation that the human condition was limited by inevitable extinction. Because the monarch linked heaven to earth it was imperative that his education be so ordered that the two bodies functioned as one, the body natural, in effect, be subordinated to the collective and mystical substance which the crown symbolized. For the well-being of the state, differentiation had to yield to integration of the bodies."

[8] Beato Juan de Avila, *Epistolario espiritual*, ed. Vicente García de Diego, Clásicos castellanos, 11 (Madrid: Ediciones de "La Lectura," 1912), p. 118. Hereafter Juan de Avila.

Carlo Mano is a ruler motivated by his egomania. Like Alonso, he allows his regard for self to override his royal duty. When he receives Alonso's letter revoking their treaty, he perceives it to be an insult to his person as well as to the King of France. His massive ego demands retribution, and he launches his attack on Spain to punish Spain and Alonso and to soothe his wounded pride. His callous sacrifice of his troops and his superior officers simply to avenge an insult demonstrate the totality of self-love and absence of regard for others.

Ximena is also intemperate. Emotionalism runs in her family. Ximena and her brother Alonso act before they think. She was evidently caught up in a highly emotional affair with Sancho and let herself be swept away by her feelings. Her intemperate and passionate behavior caused her thoughtlessly to marry Sancho without her brother's permission. Her rash behavior leads to a sequestered life in a convent.

Bernardo is the model of temperate behavior. He does not allow heated emotions to affect a reasoned approach to problem solving. His actions demonstrate that when reason is in control, rash judgments are not made. When he approaches Alonso about his plan to give the Castilian throne to France, Bernardo's insistence that Alonso realign his priorities so that the body mystical becomes more important than the body natural is an act of moderation set in opposition to immoderate and selfish behavior.

The moral vice of injustice is the direct result of intemperate behavior. Alonso's inability to control his emotions cause him to commit four unjust acts. He refuses to grant clemency to his sister; he brutally blinds her husband; he denies his nephew accession to the throne; and he schemes with the French so that Carlo Mano will become ruler of Spain.

Alonso exhibits the extent of his cruel and vengeful nature when he causes Sancho to be blinded. Cueva's purpose is to turn the spotlight upon Alonso's degradation. The visual impact upon the audience is important, for by focusing on the blinding, Cueva shows that Alonso is morally and spiritually blind to the truth. His sell-out to France serves symbolically to reinforce the understanding by the audience of the king's moral blindness.

Alonso considers himself more than just. He does not see that even as he accuses Ximena, Sancho, and Bernardo of being traitors, it is he that is the traitor. Alonso is unjust to those characters, and, through his treason, unjust to all his people. Only Bernardo is strong enough and persuasive enough to arouse Alonso's consciousness of his destructive nature. Until he decides to change his behavior, the king, who was physically chaste, falls far short of moral and spiritual chastity.

Like Alonso, Carlo Mano's intemperate nature and behavior are manifested by injustices of broad dimensions. One reason for his invasion of Spain is to satisfy his offended ego. Unlike Alonso, however, Carlo Mano is able to grasp the enormity of his injustice. Defeat of his army and the loss of three of his most valued senior officers bring an understanding of his errors of judgment and behavior. He has no Bernardo to point out his mistakes and to guide his thinking back to the golden mean; his lesson is learned the hard way through defeat and death.

Bernardo is the antithesis of Alonso and Carlo Mano as regards justice. The process by which he restores justice to the kingdom is begun by Suero and Velasco. Their loyalty to the nation and their willingness to assume the initiative are rewarded. They succeed in convincing Bernardo that he is the man capable of reversing the direction in which the monarchy is moving. Bernardo's cool logic enables him in turn to persuade Alonso to change his decision, pointing out the injustice and even treason of Alonso's agreement with Carlo Mano. Without Bernardo's sound advice, Alonso's intemperance and inequity would cost him his kingdom.

Juan de la Cueva is not subtle when he depicts this ruler whose emotional intemperance causes him to treat both his subjects and his nation unjustly. Through constant repetition of words which are semantically akin to injustice, the dramatist insures that the viewer has clearly understood his message: that intemperance and injustice are incompatible with the office of king.

Underneath this lesson in morality lies a more subtle level of meaning which is religious in nature. The themes of sin and salvation are point and counterpoint throughout, giving the play a distinctly religious foundation. The characters and the plot are bound together with these themes.

Cueva's dramatic innovation is nowhere more apparent than in his use of the themes of transgression and deliverance. Unlike some of his predecessors in the Spanish theater whose religious plays were dramatizations of events from the liturgical year, Cueva's play confronts the reason for the divine sacrifice and encompasses the core of the Christian faith. It is not surprising that Juan de la Cueva would attempt such a task, given his close association with and devotion to the church.

In *Comedia de la libertad de España por Bernardo del Carpio* Juan de la Cueva uses drama as a means of revealing to his audience a Christian truth — that redemption is always possible. Sin is a straying from God's laws. A Christian believes that reconciliation with God is possible when he takes the initiative to seek forgiveness by confessing to his sin. Hidden beneath the layers of plot which depict an individual's struggle with injustice and revenge resides the timeless Christian message: he who sins and then repents will receive God's absolution. This is the *raison d'etre* — the movement-of-spirit — of Cueva's play.

The theme of sin is centered around Alonso. During the sixteenth century it was believed that a monarch was an imitator of Christ.[9] As such he was expected to follow Christian precepts in the execution of his office. Those precepts were based on the two commandments which Christ gave his disciples: to love God totally and to love one's neighbor as self.

Alonso does not live his life pursuant to those commandments. While he pays lip service to loving God, he does not pretend to love his subjects as himself. He believes that his actions are beyond reproach and that God is on his side. When Ximena informs her brother that God will punish him for treating her so cruelly, Alonso responds that he is performing a favor for Heaven (ll. 110-114). That he believes he is doing God's will is emphasized in lines 273-280, when Alonso calls on God, the Old Testament Lord of Vengeance, to punish both Ximena and Sancho. Alonso reveals that he considers himself beyond reproach when he states, at lines 335-336, that even the king's shadow and the ground upon which he walks must be venerated. Alonso shows how callous he is when he ignores the blinded Sancho's cry that God will punish him for using such brutal means of punishment.

By the end of the second act of the play, Alonso has effectively overstepped his limits as a Christian monarch. He has permitted intemperate conceit to dominate his life to the extent that he becomes vengeful. Vengeance accounts for a major part of his decision to deny Bernardo accession to the throne (ll. 750-752). In his egomania Alonso usurps the power that rightfully belongs to God. He takes vengeance into his own hands rather than leaving it to the Lord, as he is Biblically enjoined to do. Also, he repays evil with evil,

---

[9] For further information on christomimesis (kings as imitators of Christ) and its relation to kingship see Kantorowicz, pp. 46-47: "The kings whom the Anonymous refers to are the *christi*, the anointed kings of the Old Testament, who have been foreshadowing the advent of the true royal *Christus*, the Anointed of Eternity. After the advent of Christ in the flesh, and after his ascension and exaltation as King of Glory, the terrestrial kingship underwent, very consistently, a change and received its proper function within the economy of salvation. The kings of the New Covenant no longer would appear as the 'foreshadowers' of Christ, but rather as the shadows, the imitators of Christ. The Christian ruler became the *christomimetes* — literally the 'actor' or 'impersonator' of Christ — who on the terrestrial stage presented the living image of the two-natured God, even with regard to the two unconfused natures."

contrary to St. Paul's admonition.[10] Juan de Avila writes that vengeance, compassion, and mercy in a ruler are appropriate:

> . . .castigar sin amor cerca está de vengança, o de crueldad, o dureza de coraçón, y por esto muy más lexos del castigo cristiano. El hombre deve compassión a otro hombre, y aunque la justicia le compela a lo mal tractar, no tiene liciencia para desnudar sus entrañas de compassión y misericordia para el que es hombre como él, y que, como aquel cayó, pudiera caer quien lo juzga en aquel delicto o en otros, y por ventura ha caido. Y el cristiano, cuya virtud muy principal es la misericordia, y tan embevida en su coraçón que se diga tener entrañas de misericordia, en todo deve mezclar esta virtud, conociendo que por misericordia fue él criado de nada, fue hecho cristiano, no fue condenado quando peccó, fue perdonado quando se convirtió, es tenido en pie para no tornar a caer, y en fin espera ser salvo por la misericordia de Dios; . . .[11]

Alonso imposed cruel and vengeful punishment, not Christian punishment. Mercy and compassion were not parts of his constitution; and this king would never have thought he could fall into errors made by ordinary men.

Carlo Mano is Alonso's counterpart. The French king is also guilty of the sin of egocentricity. He is the most powerful ruler in Europe and considers himself superior to the Spanish and therefore invincible. He undertakes the conquest of Spain to enlarge his power, as well as for revenge of a broken promise that would have given him that power.

When after the battle he sees his best commanders dead before him, the realization that he has sinned strikes Carlo Mano with crushing force. He divines that severe though his punishment may be, it was not so dreadful as the madness which drove him to Spain (ll. 1773-1774). The French ruler understands that Heaven had been merciful to him by granting him life and freedom to return home (ll. 1794-1796).

The two kings represent the sin of pride on a high social level. Count Tibalte represents self-interest at a lower social level. Tibalte also loves himself more than he loves his neighbor. Try as he might, he can only put himself first. His debates with his conscience could have been wrenching struggles, but they fell short of that. One voice tells him that he must help his friend and

---

10 Romans 14: 17-19.

11 Juan de Avila, p. 118.

another that he must not go against the orders of his ruler. Tibalte's decision to carry out the king's command is based ultimately upon self-interest, and he does not seem to have second thoughts or regrets. His moral dilemma is resolved in favor of the sin of self-love.

Ximena and Sancho are also guilty of the sin of selfishness. Ximena is engrossed with her feelings for Sancho to the extent that she can think of nothing but her own tormented state. Ximena seems to enjoy being the victim in the bout with her emotions when she calls it a *sabroso tormento*. Sancho's apparent lack of concern for his wife Ximena and his son Bernardo would also seem to indicate a self-centeredness.

Suero and Velasco set good examples of Christian behavior. They put love for Sancho and for the country above their own self-interest. They represent the Christian who is willing to take great risks for his beliefs. Their conviction that their friend Sancho and that their nation must be saved from a tyrannical king lead them to seek the aid of the nuns, Maria Meléndez and Urraca Sánchez. The fact that they are nuns suggests to Cueva's audience that their behavior will be beyond reproach. They are compelled by their love of Sancho, for the country, and for truth to reveal to Bernardo the severe and cruel punishment of his parents.

Suero, Velasco, and the nuns, subsequently joined by Bernardo, all understand that the king must be made to change his mind for the good of the nation and for the freedom of the people. Their plan, if successful, will force Alonso to retreat from his obstinate and treasonable posture, and also if successful, will lead him to repentance. The young man is adamant that his uncle turn from his aberrant behavior as God's representative in Spain; and, as the king, act with justice, mercy, and compassion toward the nation and the people.

Alonso yields to Bernardo's entreaties. In so doing, Alonso repents of his treason and thus in effect confesses his sins against Spain and against Bernardo by his earlier denial of accession to the throne. Subsequently the king's yielding to Bernardo's pleas for Sancho shows repentance for his cruelty to the count. If grace pardons sins which are confessed and repented, Alonso is pardoned; and it is Bernardo, aided by the grandees and the nuns, who is the intermediary of deliverance of Spain and of Sancho, and the instrument of redemption of Alonso.

Cueva now shifts the emphasis from Alonso to Carlo Mano. Bernardo is the agent who brings about his punishment for his failure to be a Christian monarch. Carlo Mano's repentance is obvious. He sees that his behavior has caused great sorrow for himself and for his nation and repents. He is absolved and is allowed to return to France alive.

Cueva ends the play with an affirmation. When Bernardo is crowned with laurel at the close of the play, Cueva is reassuring his audience that there is hope. In spite of sin and error in the world, God has not forgotten his promise of salvation. Evil has not won, nor will it win, because of God's redeeming love for His Creation.

Conclusion

The thematic structure of *Comedia de la libertad de España por Bernardo del Carpio* reveals that Juan de la Cueva did more than present history on the stage. The play is an affirmation of patriotic zeal, moral virtues and religious precepts. Cueva uses a series of contrasts as teaching devices. He moves from an old era to a new one, a new beginning for Alonso, for Carlo Mano, and for Spain. Oppression is replaced by liberty; injustice, by justice; self-love, by Christian love; disorder, by order; the darkness of sin, by the light of forgiveness.

Viewed from the moral and religious stance, the title which Cueva chose for this play assumes a secondary and symbolic meaning. "Liberty" represents freedom not only from the French invader but also from moral vices and from religious transgression. By investing this drama with important lessons to live by, Cueva hoped to teach and persuade. While his heavy-handed writing may have prevented total success, he pioneered for the Spanish theater the technique of instruction and advocacy.

Epilogue

Comedia de la libertad de España por Bernardo del Carpio best exemplifies the pivotal role played by the dramatist-poet, Juan de la Cueva, in the Spanish theater prior to Lope de Vega. Each of the pioneering efforts by Cueva — use of medieval chronicles and ballads for source material, use of polymetrical verse forms, disregard for the unities of time and place, and the use of drama to persuade — finds significant expression in this play about a medieval hero whose courage and steadfastness saved a nation and his own father, and in the doing, his king.

Cueva's style is highly rhetorical, and, while the lines are occasionally lyrical, at times the play itself becomes pedestrian. The drama could have appealed only to an educated elite, accustomed to such pomposity. If the literati did indeed value the decorous rhetoric, their regard was not sufficient to make theatrical history at the ticket window.

Without specific regard to rhetoric and versification, Cueva was successful in developing schemes at different levels of meaning. The most readily apparent scheme was that of patriotism. Any Spaniard to read or view the play would be struck by the show of love of country and the display of military strength. At another level, Cueva used his personal and more subtle patriotism to attempt to warn his own sovereign, Philip II, against an invasion of Portugal. History records that he failed in that effort; and later history suggests the wisdom and foresight of the author.

Cueva also addressed the individual with themes grounded in morals and religion. The moral themes emphasize the importance of virtuous living, suggesting that intemperance and often resultant injustice must be avoided. The parallel religious themes form the real foundation of the play. In one vein, Cueva has his characters calling upon Heaven or God to accomplish things, and the viewer can easily distinguish the lessons of Alonso calling upon God to punish his enemies, of Bernardo calling upon Alonso to recall God's compassion, and of Carlo Mano's anguished acknowledgment of God's hand in his defeat. In the other vein, Cueva exemplifies good and evil, God and Satan, sin and repentance through adroit characterization.

Cueva's importance in the evolving Spanish theater should not be underestimated. His influence upon subsequent Spanish dramatists becomes apparent not only in the technical aspects of writing a play, but also in the aesthetics of creating drama. Therein lies Cueva's contribution to Hispanic belles-lettres; and nowhere is his contribution displayed with clearer definition than in *Comedia de la libertad de España por Bernardo del Carpio*.

Appendix A

Examples of Juan de la Cueva's Spelling Style

1) Frequent omission of initial H:
ay, e dado, onesto
but hecho, herir
2) Consistent use of medial RR:
honrra, honrró, arrogancia
3) Consistent use of medial SS:
assolar, assí, desseada
4) Vacilation between V, B:
rebuelto, bolved, deve, iva
vozes, bozes
5) Vacilation between medial J, X:
trabajosa, consejo, dexada, dixo, truxo
6) Consistent use of Ç after consonants:
esperança, fuerça
7) Vacilation between Ç, Z after vowels:
estrañeza, dezir, braço, empeçado
8) Q for C before UA:
qual, quan, esquadra
9) Consistent use of apostrophe for final E before following vowel:
qu'estimo, d'estar, m'obliga, entr'ellos
10) Assimilation of RL to LL:
estorvallo, deshazello, buscallo
11) Other examples of orthographic archaisms:
triumphar, só, magestad, comigo, immortal, obscuro

Appendix B

Tabulation of Verse Forms in
Comedia de la libertad de España por Bernardo del Carpio

Jornada I	
octava (ABABABCC)	1 - 56
redondilla (abba)	57 - 264
octava	265 - 336
Jornada II	
estancia (ABCBACcDeeDFdF) (14-line stanzas)	337 - 392
redondilla	393 - 456
octava	457 - 552
redondilla	553 - 704
Jornada III	
terceto (ABA BCB CDC)	705 - 762
octava	763 - 898
redondilla	899 - 994
octava	995 - 1106
redondilla	1107 - 1218
octava	1219 - 1298

Jornada IV

octava	1299 - 1386
redondilla	1387 - 1434
octava	1435 - 1466
redondilla	1467 - 1570
octava	1571 - 1770
estancia (ABCBACcDEeDFF) (13-line stanzas)	1771 - 1809
redondilla	1810 - 1849
octava	1850 - 1873

Recapitulation

octava	896 lines	48%
redondilla	824 lines	44%
estancia	95 lines	5%
terceto	58 lines	3%

Appendix C

Epistola dedicatoria a Momo (1583)

Vna delas cosas (antiguo Momo) que los sabios dela antiguedad estimaron en gran veneracion, fue la virtud dela Tēplança, a quiē atribuyeron entre las demas virtudes gran excelencia, considerando que la perficiō de todas consistia en la obseruacion della, i de aqui vino el ennoblecerse las Republicas, ensancharse las Monarquias, i avn el eternizarse los hombres de tal suerte, que menos preciaron la velocidad del Tiempo, aquellos que con eficaz perseuerancia la siguieron. Porque demas de las muchas experiencias que tiene, es abraçada (segun dize Ciceron) dela Fortaleza, Iusticia, i Prudencia como de quiē las demas virtudes son gouernadas. Esto no fue tan general q no padeciesse excecion, que en estos tiempos (quādo fue la Templança no menos que deidad reuerenciada) dexasse de ser desconocida; i sino lo fue, no seguida ni estimada de muchos que desenfrenadamente se apartaron de sus onestos medios, siguiendo los viciosos estremos. Porque el poderoso era intolerable, el noble altiuo, el fuerte soberuio, el rico vanaglorioso, el Iuez sin clemencia, iel sabio maldiziente. Esta plaga a redūdado desde aquellos tiempos hasta los nuestros, i de tal suerte a tendido sus contagiosos ramos, que todo es señoreado i a vn contaminado dela horrible murmuraciō sin essentar ni aun las cosas que entre los Antiguos fueron sagradas, i de nosotros dinamente por exemplar de virtud tenidas. Cuyo tiranico rigor tiene tan opresos los animos virtuosos, q no ai a quien no le falte, ni quien tenga valor para hazer demostracion de cosas de ingenio ni virtud, temiendo (o mordaz Momo) tu venenoso contagio, cuyo miedo con mui justa razon, causa al Mundo espanto. i a sido en mi tan poderoso, que siendome forçado por mui ligitimas cavsas sacar a luz esse libro, è andado vacilando no pocos dias en hazer lo que a de serme reputado a temeridad, conociendo la insuficiencia mia, i tu horrible condicion, i disponerme a emprender tal hazaña con tan debiles fuerças como las mias. I al fin siendo mas poderosa la cavsa, que la resistencia, vine forçadamente a condecender, i a poner en execucion lo que fue de mi con tanta razõ temido, i a darte materia en que se emprenda la llama de tu detracion, i aliento para que tu natural costũbre execute su crueldad. Por que con gran dificultad se puede apartar de vna larga costumbre, que està ya cõuertida casi en naturaleza, i al estomago mal dispuesto qualquier manjar es desabrido, imas al tuyo, a quien ningun gusto se lo dio jamas, aunque fuesse de Nectar, i ofrecerle assi essas Comedias i Tragedias, es cosa que ya que no es condenada por mala, parecera á los Inorantes que es indigna de ser acepta i estimada en gran veneracion, delos que siguen las honrrosas letras, i exercitan la loable virtud, yerro por cierto no dino de perdon, i de ser condenado por Inorante el que osare ocupar la imaginacion en tal inorancia, pues consta quantos i quan excelentes ombres, assi ennobleza de sangre, en potestad de Fortuna, i en eminencia de letras, se ocuparõ en este genero de escritura, i compusierõ muchas Comedias i Tragedias sin desdeñarse de sacarlas a los Teatros a ser representadas en sus nombres, teniendo el exercicio dellas por principal virtud. I à llegado la malicia de nuestros tiempos en algunos, a querer formar escrupulo de afrenta en la composicion dellas, sin considerar el prouecho que enla republica resulta de su letura, Pues la Comedia esimitacion de la Vida humana, espejo de las costumbres, retrato dela verdad, en que se nos representan las cosas que devemos huir, o las que nos conviene elegir, con claros i evidentes exemplos poderoso qualquiera dellos à confundir las cauilosas intenciones, delos que condenan este genero de Poesia, enel qual temiendo solo lo que a mi parte toca, i estando convencido a comunicar esse Libro, aviendo investigado con la imaginacion a quien pudiesse dedicarlo, que lo defendiesse del Tiempo, i su memoria hiziesse eterna, hallè que solo a ti pertenece la dedicaciõ del, como a Principe delos maldiziẽtes, i tenido de la gentilidad por el Dios dellos, i que siguiendo tu natural costumbre, diràs contra el tantas, i tales cosas, las quales esparzidas por el Mundo, forçosamente vendra a ser eterno por el camino que tu pretẽderás desuiarlo de la memoria de los hõbres, i sepultallo en las tinieblas del Oluido; Aunque para ser ofendido de ti, i delos que siguen tu parcialidad, aya sido de poco efecto acercarlo tanto a tu presencia, pues n[o ay] lugar por apartado que estẽ, a donde no llegue tu mano, ni Deidad aquiẽ reserue tu lẽgua por justificada qu[e sea] pues eres Fiscal de justos, i de injustos, de viuos i mu[ertos,] Cẽsor delos vnos i delos otros, i Detractor avn delos mes[mos] Dioses.

Con todo esto considerando (sino es falta mi consideracion) que seras de la calidad del perro, q no muerde al que se le echa a los pies, quise dirigirlo a tu nombre, i ponerlo en tu mano, por obligarte a que desmientas las espias, i que ya no seas en defendello, por no ir contra tu costumbre, moderes la ira de tu mordaz rigor en su ofensa, viendo la voluntad con que se te ofrece, i la poca defensa que de mi parte tiene, i si nada desto no te mouiere (porque segun dize Platõ no ai cosa que casi prometa imposibilidad como la mudança de vna especie enotra) desuia de ti la ciega passion, i considera, reboluiendo essas Comedias, i Tragedias, la variedad de cosas de tanto gusto q en ellas hallaràs, assi de hechos eroicos de esclarecidos Varones, como castissimos amores de constantes mugeres, sin otros muchos exemplos, que dinamente lo puedẽ ser de nuestra vida, aquien no podra la inuidiosa murmuracion, enemiga de toda virtud, ofender si no es desuiandose dela razon Iusticia, i Templança, qual tienen de costumbre los que siguẽ tan abominable uso, cuyo parecer no es aprouado del justo, ni yo lo procuro, porque no se puede disputar delealtad conel Traidor, deletras con el ignorãte ni de piedad conel Tirano.

Vale

Bibliography

Alfonso X, el Sabio. Las quatro partes enteras de la Cronica de Espana que mando Componer el Serenissimo rey don Alfonso llamado el sabio, Uista y emendada mucha parte de su impresion por el maestro Florian Docampo. Zamora: Agustin de Paz y Juan Picardo, 1541.

__________. *Primera crónica general de España.* Ed. Ramón Menéndez Pidal. 2d. ed. 2 vols. Madrid: Editorial Gredos, 1955.

Avila, Beato Juan de. *Epistolario espiritual,* Ed. Vicente García de Diego. Clásicos castellanos, 11. Madrid: Ediciones de "La Lectura," 1912.

Battle, John W. "Dramatic Unity in the Plays of Juan de la Cueva." Diss. Duke University 1970.

Bullfinch, Thomas. *Legends of Charlemagne*. London: J. M. Dent; New York: E. P. Dutton, 1924.

Burton, David G. "Virtue Triumphant in Cueva's *La libertad de España por Bernardo del Carpio.*" *Bulletin of the Comediantes,* 38 (1986), 219-29.

Cebrián García, José. *La fábula de Marte y Venus de Juan de la Cueva. Significación y sentido.* Sevilla: Publicaciones de la Universidad de Sevilla, 1986.

__________, ed. *Juan de la Cueva. Fábulas mitológicas y épica burlesca.* Madrid: Editora Nacional, 1984.

__________. "Juan de la Cueva, Traductor de la (Batracomiomaquia)." *Revista de literatura,* 47, 93 (1985), pp. 23-39.

__________. "Nuevos datos para las biografías del inquisidor Claudio de la Cueva (1551?-1611) y del poeta Juan de la Cueva (1543-1612) I." *Archivo Hispalense,* 202 (1983), 3-29.

Cueva, Juan de la. *La libertad de España por Bernardo del Carpio*. Ed. Anthony Watson. Exeter Hispanic Texts, Number 8. Exeter, England: University Printing Unit, 1974.

__________. *Comedias i tragedias*. Sevilla: Andrea Pescioni, 1583.

__________. *Comedias y tragedias*. Ed. Francisco A. de Icaza. 2 vols. Madrid: Sociedad de Bibliófilos Españoles, 1917.

__________. *Historia y sucesión de la Cueva*. In *Archivo Hispalense*, 1 (1886), 261-72, 290-309; 2 (1886), 17-24, 41-48, 65-72, 87-96.

__________. *El Infamador, Los siete Infantes de Lara, Exemplar poético*. Ed. Francisco A. de Icaza. Clásicos castellanos, 60. Madrid: Espasa-Calpe, 1924.

Davies, R. Trevor. *The Golden Century of Spain 1501-1621*. London: Macmillan and Co., 1937.

Domínguez Ortiz, Antonio. *Orto y ocaso de Sevilla*. 3a. ed. Colección de bolsillo, número 31. Sevilla: Universidad de Sevilla, 1981.

Durán, Agustín, ed. *Romancero general o Colección de romances castellanos anteriores al siglo XVIII*. Biblioteca de Autores Españoles, 10. Madrid: Atlas, 1945.

Enciclopedia Universal Ilustrada. Madrid: Espasa-Calpe, 1907?-30.

Entwistle, William J. "The 'Cantar de Gesta' of Bernardo del Carpio." *Modern Language Review*, 23 (1928), 307-22, 432-52.

Franklin, Albert B. III. "A Study of the Origins of the Legend of Bernardo del Carpio." *Hispanic Review*, 5 (1937), 286-303.

__________. "The Origin of the Legend of Bernardo del Carpio." Diss. Harvard 1938.

Froldi, Rinaldo. *Lope de Vega y la formación de la comedia*. Salamanca: Anaya, 1973.

Gallardo, Bartolomé José. *Ensayo de una biblioteca de libros raros y curiosos*. 4 vols. Madrid: Imprenta y Estereotipia de M. Rivadeneyra, 1863-89.

Glenn, Richard F. *Juan de la Cueva*. New York: Twayne Publishers, 1973.

Hämel, Adalbert. *Der Cid im spanischen Drama des XVI und XVII Jahrhunderts*. Halle: n.p., 1910.

__________. "Sobre la primera edición de las obras dramáticas de Juan de la Cueva." *Revista de Filología Española*, 10 (1923), 182-3.

Hayes, Francis C. *Lope de Vega*. New York: Twayne Publishers, 1967.

Heinermann, Theodor. *Untersuchungen zur Entstehung der Sage von Bernardo del Carpio*. Halle (Saale): Max Niemeyer, 1927.

Kamen, Henry. *The Spanish Inquisition*. New York: The New American Library, 1965.

Kantorowicz, Ernst. *The King's Two Bodies: A Study in Medieval Political Theory*. Princeton: Princeton University Press, 1957.

King, Willard F. "The Academies and Seventeenth-Century Spanish Literature." *PMLA*, 75 (1960), 367-76.

Lázaro Carreter, Fernando. *Lope de Vega. Introducción a su vida y obra*. Salamanca: Anaya, 1966.

López Morales, Humberto. *Tradición y creación en los orígenes del teatro castellano*. Madrid: Ediciones Alcalá, 1968.

Lucas de Tuy. *Chronicon mundi*. See Heinermann.

__________. *Crónica de España*. Ed. Julio Puyol. Madrid: Tipografía de la Revista de Archivos, Bibliotecas y Museos, 1926.

McCrary, William C. "Ritual Action and Form in *La Estrella de Sevilla*." In *Homenaje a William L. Fichter: Estudios sobre el teatro antiguo hispánico y otros ensayos*. Madrid: Editorial Castalia, 1971, pp. 505-13.

Menéndez Pidal, Ramón, ed. *Romancero tradicional de las lenguas hispánicas (español-portugués-catalán-sefardí)*. 2 vols. Madrid: Editorial Gredos, 1957.

Menéndez y Pelayo, Marcelino. "*Las mocedades de Bernardo del Carpio*." In *Estudios sobre el teatro de Lope de Vega*, vol. 31 in *Edición nacional de las obras completas de Menéndez Pelayo*. Madrid: Consejo Superior de Investigaciones Científicas, 1949.

Milá y Fontanals, Manuel. *De la poesía heroico-popular castellana*. Barcelona: Librería de Alvaro Verdaguer, 1874.

Montero, Juan. "Otro ataque contra las anotaciones herrerianas: La epístola 'A Cristóbal de Sayas de Alfaro' de Juan de la Cueva." *Revista de literatura*, 48, 95 (1986), pp. 19-33.

Moratín, Leandro Fernández de. *Orígenes del teatro español*. Buenos Aires: Editorial Schapire, 1946.

Morby, Edwin Seth. "Notes on Juan de la Cueva: Versification and Dramatic Theory." *Hispanic Review*, 8 (1940), 213-18.

__________. "The Plays of Juan de la Cueva." Diss. University of California 1936.

Ocampo, Florián de. See Alfonso X, el Sabio. Las quatro partes enteras dela Crónica de España.

Oliveira Marques, A. H. de. *History of Portugal*. New York and London: Columbia University Press, 1972.

Pike, Ruth. *Aristocrats and Traders. Sevillian Society in the Sixteenth Century*. Ithaca: Cornell University Press, 1972.

Poema de Fernán González. Ed. Alonso Zamora Vicente. Clásicos castellanos, 128. Madrid: Espasa-Calpe, 1970.

Porrata, Francisco E. *Incorporación del romancero a la temática de la comedia española*. Madrid: Editorial Playor, 1973.

Rada, Rodrigo Ximénez de. *De rebus Hispaniae*. In Elio Antonio de Nebrija, Habes in hoc volvmine amice lector. Aelii Antonii Nebrissensis Rervm a Fernando & Elisabe Hispaniarum foelicissimis Regibus gestar Decades duae. Necnon belli Nauariensis libros duos. Annexa insuper Archiepiscopi Roderici Chronica, aliisque historiis antehac non excussis. Granatam: [Xanthos Nebrisenses], 1545.

Rennert, Hugo A. *The Life of Lope de Vega (1562-1635)*. 1904; rpt. New York: G. E. Stechert & Co., 1937.

Reyes Cano, José María. "Documentos relativos a Juan de la Cueva: Nuevos datos para su biografía." *Archivo Hispalense*, 196 (1981), 107-35.

__________. *La poesía lírica de Juan de la Cueva*. Sevilla: Publicaciones de la Excma. Diputación Provincial de Sevilla, 1980.

Rodríguez Marín, Francisco. *Nuevos datos para las biografías de cien escritores de los siglos XVI y XVII*. Madrid: Tipografía de la Revista de Archivos, Bibliotecas y Museos, 1923.

Rodríguez-Moñino, Antonio. *Manual bibliográfico de cancioneros y romanceros*. Madrid: Editorial Castalia, 1973.

Rosaldo, Renato. "*Flores de baria poesía*. Apuntes preliminares para el estudio de un cancionero manuscrito mexicano del XVI." *Hispania*, 34 (1951), 177-80.

__________. "*Flores de baria poesía*. Estudio preliminar de un cancionero inédito mexicano de 1577." *Abside*, 15, No. 3 (julio-sept., 1951), 373-96; No. 4 (oct.-dic., 1951), 523-50; 16, No. 1 (enero-marzo, 1952), 91-122.

Sedano, Juan Joseph López de, ed. *Parnaso español. Colección de poesías escogidas de los más célebres poetas castellanos*. 9 vols. Madrid: Antonio de Sancha, 1770-1778.

Verdevoye, Paul. "Le poème 'Llanto de Venus en la muerte de Adonis' de Juan de la Cueva dans sa version définitive en partie inédite." *Bulletin Hispanique*, 64 bis (1962), 677-89.

Watson, Anthony. *Juan de la Cueva and the Portuguese Succession*. London: Tamesis Books, 1971.

Weiss, Beno, and Louis C. Pérez. *Juan de la Cueva's Los Inventores de las*

Cosas. University Park, Pa.: Pennsylvania State University Press, 1980.

Wulff, Fredrik A. "Poèmes inédits de Juan de la Cueva." *Lunds Universitets Ars-skrift*, 23 (1886-87), pp. i-c, 1-64.

Scripta humanistica

Directed by
BRUNO M. DAMIANI
The Catholic University of America
*COMPREHENSIVE LIST OF PUBLICATIONS**

1.	Everett W. Hesse, *The "Comedia" and Points of View.*	$24.50
2.	Marta Ana Diz, *Patronio y Lucanor: la lectura inteligente "en el tiempo que es turbio."* Prólogo de John Esten Keller.	$26.00
3.	James F. Jones, Jr., *The Story of a Fair Greek of Yesteryear.* A Translation from the French of Antoine-François Prévost's *L'Histoire d'une Grecque moderne.* With Introduction and Selected Bibliography.	$30.00
4.	Colette H. Winn, *Jean de Sponde: Les sonnets de la mort ou La Poétique de l'accoutumance.* Préface par Frédéric Deloffre.	out of print
5.	Jack Weiner, *"En busca de la justicia social: estudio sobre el teatro español del Siglo de Oro."*	$24.50
6.	Paul A. Gaeng, *Collapse and Reorganization of the Latin Nominal Flection as Reflected in Epigraphic Sources.* Written with the assistance of Jeffrey T. Chamberlin.	$24.00
7.	Edna Aizenberg, *The Aleph Weaver: Biblical, Kabbalistic, and Judaic Elements in Borges.*	$25.00
8.	Michael G. Paulson and Tamara Alvarez-Detrell, *Cervantes, Hardy, and "La fuerza de la sangre."*	$25.50
9.	Rouben Charles Cholakian, *Deflection/Reflection in the Lyric Poetry of Charles d'Orléans: A Psychosemiotic Reading.*	$25.00
10.	Kent P. Ljungquist, *The Grand and the Fair: Poe's Landscape Aesthetics and Pictorial Techniques.*	out of print
11.	D.W. McPheeters, *Estudios humanísticos sobre la "Celestina."*	$20.00
12.	Vittorio Felaco, *The Poetry and Selected Prose of Camillo Sbarbaro.* Edited and Translated by Vittorio Felaco. With a Preface by Franco Fido.	$25.00
13.	María del C. Candau de Cevallos, *Historia de la lengua española.*	$33.00
14.	*Renaissance and Golden Age Studies in Honor of D.W. McPheeters.* Ed. Bruno M. Damiani.	out of print
15.	Bernardo Antonio González, *Parábolas de identidad: Realidad interior y estrategia narrativa en tres novelistas de postguerra.*	$28.00
16.	Carmelo Gariano, *La Edad Media (Aproximación Alfonsina).*	$30.00
17.	Gabriella Ibieta, *Tradition and Renewal in "La gloria de don Ramiro".*	$27.50
18.	*Estudios literarios en honor de Gustavo Correa.* Eds. Charles Faulhaber, Richard Kinkade, T.A. Perry. Preface by Manuel Durán.	$25.00
19.	George Yost, *Pieracci and Shelly: An Italian Ur-Cenci.*	$27.50

20. Zelda Irene Brooks, *The Poetry of Gabriel Celaya.* $26.00
21. *La relación o naufragios de Alvar Núñez Cabeza de Vaca,* eds. Martin A. Favata y José B. Fernández. $27.50
22. Pamela S. Brakhage, *The Theology of "La Lozana andaluza."* $27.50
23. Jorge Checa, *Gracián y la imaginación arquitectónica.* $28.00
24. Gloria Gálvez Lira, *Maria Luisa Bombal: Realidad y Fantasía.* $28.50
25. Susana Hernández Araico, *Ironía y tragedia en Calderón.* $25.00
26. Philip J. Spartano, *Giacomo Zanella: Poet, Essayist, and Critic of the "Risorgimento."* Preface by Roberto Severino. out of print
27. E. Kate Stewart, *Arthur Sherburne Hardy: Man of American Letters.* Preface by Louis Budd. $28.50
28. Giovanni Boccaccio, *The Decameron.* English Adaptation by Carmelo Gariano. $30.00
29. Giacomo A. Striuli, "Alienation in Giuseppe Berto". $26.50
30. Barbara Mujica, *Iberian Pastoral Characters.* Preface by Frederick A. de Armas. $33.00
31. Susan Niehoff McCrary, "*'El último godo' and the Dynamics of the Urdrama.*" Preface by John E. Keller. $27.50
32. *En torno al hombre y a sus monstruos: Ensayos críticos sobre la novelística de Carlos Rojas,* editados por Cecilia Castro Lee y C. Christopher Soufas, Jr. $31.50
33. J. Thomas O'Connell, *Mount Zion Field.* $24.50
34. Francisco Delicado, *Portrait of Lozana: The Lusty Andalusian Woman.* Translation, introduction and notes by Bruno M. Damiani. $45.50
35. Elizabeth Sullam, *Out of Bounds.* Foreword by Michael G. Cooke. $23.50
36. Sergio Corsi, *Il "modus digressivus" nella "Divina Commedia"* $28.75
37. Juan Bautista Avalle-Arce, *Lecturas (Del temprano Renacimiento a Valle Inclán).* $28.50
38. Rosendo Díaz-Peterson, *Las novelas de Unamuno.* Prólogo de Antonio Carreño. $30.00
39. Jeanne Ambrose, *Syntaxe Comparative Français-Anglais.* $29.50
40. Nancy Marino, *La serranilla española: notas para su historia e interpretación.* $28.75.
41. Carolyn Kreiter-Kurylo, *Contrary Visions.* Preface by Peter Klappert. $24.50
42. Giorgio Perissinotto, *Reconquista y literatura medieval: Cuatro Ensayos.* $29.50
43. Rick Wilson, *Between a Rock and a Heart Place.* $25.00
44. *Feminine Concerns in Contemporary Spanish Fiction by Women.* Edited by Roberto C. Manteiga, Carolyn Galerstein and Kathleen McNerney. $35.00
45. Pierre L. Ullman, *A Contrapuntal Method For Analyzing Spanish Literature.* $41.50
46. Richard D. Woods, *Spanish Grammar and Culture Through Proverbs.* $35.00

47. David G. Burton, *The Legend of Bernardo del Carpio. From Chronicle to Drama*. Preface by John Lihani. $30.00
48. Godwin Okebaram Uwah, *Pirandellism and Samuel Beckett's Plays*. $28.00
49. *Italo-Hispanic Literary Relations*, ed. J. Helí Hernández. $33.00
50. *Studies in Honor of Elias Rivers*, eds. Bruno M. Damiani and Ruth El Saffar. $30.00

BOOK ORDERS

* Clothbound. *All book orders*, except library orders, must be prepaid and addressed to **Scripta Humanistica**, 1383 Kersey Lane, Potomac, Maryland 20854. *Manuscripts* to be considered for publication should be sent to the same address.

www.ingramcontent.com/pod-product-compliance
Lightning Source LLC
Chambersburg PA
CBHW020941310726
48980CB00001B/7

* 9 7 8 0 1 9 6 3 7 9 5 4 8 *